T0224373

Lecture Notes in Computer Science 8355

Commenced Publication in 1973
Founding and Former Series Editors:
Gerhard Goos, Juris Hartmanis, and Jan van Leeuwen

Marinos Ioannides   Ewald Quak (Eds.)

3D Research Challenges in Cultural Heritage

A Roadmap in Digital Heritage Preservation

Volume Editors

Marinos Ioannides
Cyprus University of Technology
Department of Electrical and Computer Engineering and Informatics
Digital Heritage Research Lab
Archbishop Kyprianou 31
3036 Limassol, Cyprus
E-mail: marinos.ioannides@cut.ac.cy

Ewald Quak
Tallinn University of Technology
Institute of Cybernetics
Wave Engineering Laboratory
Center for Nonlinear Studies
Akadeemia tee 21, 12618 Tallinn, Estonia
E-mail: ewald.quak@cs.ioc.ee

ISSN 0302-9743   e-ISSN 1611-3349
ISBN 978-3-662-44629-4   e-ISBN 978-3-662-44630-0
DOI 10.1007/978-3-662-44630-0
Springer Heidelberg New York Dordrecht London

Library of Congress Control Number: 2014947729

LNCS Sublibrary: SL 3 – Information Systems and Application,
incl. Internet/Web and HCI

Typesetting: Camera-ready by author, data conversion by Scientific Publishing Services, Chennai, India

Printed on acid-free paper

Springer is part of Springer Science+Business Media (www.springer.com)

3D Research Challenges in Cultural Heritage Applications

Preface

Recent research and development activities in 3D technologies have led to rapid progress with far-reaching impact in numerous applications spanning very diverse areas both for highly-skilled professionals – such as computer-aided design and engineering for digital factories of the future and advanced simulators for flight and surgical training – as well as for the general public now using 3D maps and enjoying 3D TV/cinema and computer games. In general, it has turned out that the handling of 3D data poses different challenges but also provides growth for new, exciting and innovative opportunities compared to more established media like texts, images or sound.

Some 3D technologies are already being used successfully also in the cultural heritage (CH) domain, especially in the area of digital libraries for cultural heritage like Europeana (www.europeana.eu) and the UNESCO Memory of the World. A workshop on these topics was organized by the editors of this volume at the International Conference on Cultural Heritage EuroMed2012 (www.euromed2012.eu) on the island of Cyprus in October 2012. This was the official event of the Cyprus Presidency of the Council of the European Union, bringing together specialists of different 3D technologies and cultural heritage areas to present recent advances and discuss the way forward. At this workshop, the idea for this volume originated, with the intent of gathering 3D research challenges for the digital cultural heritage domain. Contributions from renowned researchers in this specific area and workshop participants have been selected. The aim of this book is to provide an insight into ongoing research and future directions in this novel, continuously evolving field, which lies at the intersection of digital heritage, engineering, computer science, material science, architecture, civil engineering, and archaeology.

Overall, in our opinion, the chapters in the book reflect the following 3D Challenges in the CH Domain:

1. Transition of CH Objects from Real to Virtual,
2. Interplay of Geometry and Semantics for CH,
3. Organization of Large 3D Databases in CH,
4. Handling 3D Data in CH over the Internet and Mobile Devices,
5. Presenting CH Content in 3D to the General Public,
6. Contributing to the Research of CH Professionals,
7. Reconstruction of CH Objects from Virtual to Real and their 3D production and use.

1. The acquisition of virtual 3D computer models, typically using laser scanning technology but also using computer-aided design, raises various problems related to the huge number of objects that should be dealt with as well as their size, material, accessibility, etc.

2. The geometric description of a CH object in some computer-tractable form is clearly distinguished from the historical description of the build, meaning and purpose of a CH object, which has been studied for centuries in areas like architecture. The story telling and the mathematical model have to be suitably interwoven.

3. Once acquired, the large set of digitally available 3D objects must be properly organized with the right metadata to allow activities like exchange and comparison not just within one institution but Europe wide for example through libraries such as Europeana or even globally integrated in GIS systems and geo-maps like Google Maps.

4. The presentation/display of 3D CH objects for users who are not IT specialists, allowing them the use and even manipulation of such objects for practical activities, poses a lot of technical questions concerning 3D web browsers, mobile devices, etc.

5. CH in 3D content can be presented to the general public in a gripping, immersive setting, capturing people's attention. This necessitates, however, the easy development of animated 3D scenes and 3D authoring tools for interactive experiences, usable by specialists for the CH content who should not have to be very familiar with IT issues.

6. 3D technologies should also help CH professionals in their daily research work, for example, assisting – literally – in the search for missing pieces in archaeological settings.

7. New 3D printing technologies allow on the one hand, the detailed reconstruction of 3D CH objects in previously unknown fidelity in shape and material and on the other hand they are finally giving laymen viable options to turn available virtual CH models into tangible real entities. This can support real CH object exhibitions of previously unseen objects and assist in the repatriation of some of these replicas back to their origin.

Naturally some of the above mentioned challenges are very well-known from other 3D application areas but may have a different twist in the CH domain. The different issues are obviously interwoven which becomes apparent when studying the chapters of this book.

The paper by Santos et.al. provides very interesting information on the sheer volume of the task of scanning 3D museum objects (Challenge 1) but also on the development of 3D web browsers (Challenge 4). The text by di Benedetto et.al. discusses web and mobile visualization (Challenge 4). The relationship of geometry and semantics (Challenge 2) is considered by Havemann et.al. concerning procedural shape modelling and by De Luca et.al. for architectural elements. Tal considers in her chapter the use of mathematical shape analysis techniques in an archaeological setting that have become part of an IT-system for archaeologists (Challenge 6). 3D issues for the reconstruction of virtual heritage scenes with large populations (Challenge 5) are the subject of the contribution by Thalmann et.al. Important lessons from the film industry, especially concerning the managing of digital assets (Challenge 3), are provided in the paper by Dodgson. The content creation (Challenge 5) is the focus of the chapter by Linaza et.al. Finally, 3D reconstruction (Challenge 7) is the topic of the contributions by Callet for a high-precision setting both in shape and material and by Neumüller et.al. for 3D printing, especially for wider audiences.

What is the way forward to further address these challenges? Another workshop at the next EuroMed2014 (www.euromed2014.eu) conference, again to be held in Cyprus in November 2014, will discuss future perspectives. The contributions in this volume show that substantial activities have been carried out in CH-related projects funded by the European Commission. The first worldwide fellowship programme funded by the Marie Curie Initial Training Network on Digital Cultural Heritage: Projecting our Past to the Future (www.itn-dch.org) is intending to train the next generation of young researchers also in 3D technologies for cultural heritage.

So in conclusion, a further challenge for the research community in Europe working on 3D technologies for cultural heritage is to systemically, creatively – and hopefully successfully – apply for funding for exciting new activities in the Horizon2020 Framework Programme. Simultaneously the European Commission should highlight cultural heritage applications in the new editions of the H2020 work program for the coming years.

Marinos Ioannides
Ewald Quak

Table of Contents

The Potential of 3D Internet in the Cultural Heritage Domain 1
   Pedro Santos, Sebastian Pena Serna, André Stork, and Dieter Fellner

Web and Mobile Visualization for Cultural Heritage 18
   Marco Di Benedetto, Federico Ponchio, Luigi Malomo,
   Marco Callieri, Matteo Dellepiane, Paolo Cignoni, and
   Roberto Scopigno

Geometry vs Semantics: Open Issues on 3D Reconstruction of
Architectural Elements 36
   Livio De Luca and David Lo Buglio

3D Shape Analysis for Archaeology 50
   Ayellet Tal

Procedural Shape Modeling in Digital Humanities: Potentials
and Issues 64
   Sven Havemann, Olaf Wagener, and Dieter Fellner

Geometric Issues in Reconstruction of Virtual Heritage Involving Large
Populations 78
   Daniel Thalmann, Barbara Maïm, and Jonathan Maïm

Going to the Movies: Lessons from the Film Industry for 3D
Libraries 93
   Neil A. Dodgson

Reusing Multimedia Content for the Creation of Interactive Experiences
in Cultural Institutions 104
   Maria Teresa Linaza, Miriam Juaristi, and Ander Garcia

3D Printing for Cultural Heritage: Preservation, Accessibility, Research
and Education 119
   Moritz Neumüller, Andreas Reichinger, Florian Rist, and
   Christian Kern

3D Reconstruction from 3D Cultural Heritage Models 135
   Patrick Callet

Author Index 143

The Potential of 3D Internet in the Cultural Heritage Domain

Pedro Santos[1], Sebastian Pena Serna[1], André Stork[1], and Dieter Fellner[2]

[1] Fraunhofer IGD, Fraunhoferstr. 5, 64283 Darmstadt, Germany
{pedro.santos,sebastian.pena.serna,
andre.stork}@igd.fraunhofer.de
[2] GRIS/TU-Darmstadt, Fraunhoferstr. 5, 64283 Darmstadt, Germany
dieter.fellner@gris.tu-darmstadt.de

Europe is rich in cultural heritage but unfortunately much of the tens of millions of artifacts remain in archives. Many of these resources have been collected to preserve our history and to understand their historical context. Nevertheless, CH institutions are neither able to document all the collected resources nor to exhibit them. Additionally, many of these CH resources are unique, and will be on public display only occasionally. Hence, access to and engagement with this kind of cultural resources is important for European culture and the legacy of future generations. However, the technology needed to economically mass digitize and annotate 3D artifacts in analogy to the digitization and annotation of books and paintings has yet to be developed. Likewise approaches to semantic enrichment and storage of 3D models along with meta-data are just emerging. This paper presents challenges and trends to overcome the latter issues and demonstrates latest developments for annotation of 3D artifacts and their subsequent export to Europeana, the European digital library, for integrated, interactive 3D visualization within regular web browsers taking advantage of technologies such as WebGl and X3D.

Keywords: Cultural heritage, digitization, 3d reconstruction, photorealistic rendering, virtual replica.

1   Introduction

The major impact of the world wide web was to enable simple and unified access to information through hyperlinks. With the first search engines, that information became annotated, so finding information became easier. Then a number of initiatives started out digitizing and annotating books and paintings to preserve cultural heritage in a digital form. Nowadays we are on the verge of digitization and annotation of 3D cultural heritage as the logical next step towards sustainable cultural heritage preservation and the main question is: Which are the technologies that allow an economical approach to mass digitization and annotation of 3D cultural heritage?

Our museums and cultural institutions are home to millions of cultural heritage artifacts. The collection of the Prussian Cultural Heritage Foundation in Berlin and its multiple museums alone is estimated to amount to 6 million artifacts of which only

M. Ioannides and E. Quak (Eds.): 3D Research Challenges, LNCS 8355, pp. 1–17, 2014.

10% are presented to the public, while 90% remain archived and eventually "undiscovered". An enormous amount of cultural heritage artifacts are 3D objects such as statues, busts, coins, pottery or archaeological findings. Yet so far, economical digitization on a large scale has only been implemented for 2D cultural heritage artifacts such as antique books and paintings, initiated by multiple national, European and international campaigns, some of the most prominent actors being the Europeana, the German Digital Library and the Google and Microsoft library projects. The market for digitization service providers and device manufacturers is estimated at around 100 million Euro.

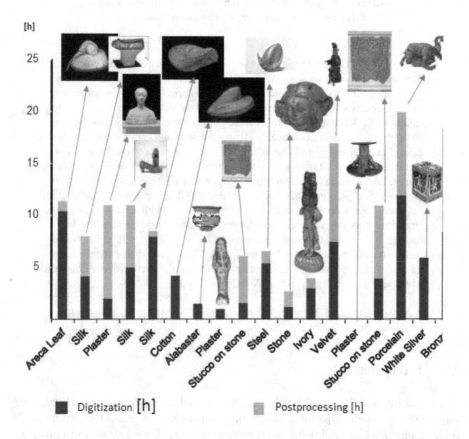

Fig. 1. Digitization campaign conducted by the V&A Museum – more than 40 objects being scanned. Time varies between 5 and 20 hours for geometry and texture only – no complex material acquisition included. Scanner used: Breuckmann optoTOP-HE. Red bars indicate the acquisition time and green bars the post-processing time.

The 3D digitization market of cultural heritage artifacts has not yet been explored to its full potential while it offers many advantages such as:

- Arbitrary availability and parallel access to digital replicas of cultural heritage artifacts
- Use of realistic 3D models for documentation, exhibition and acquisition planning
- Virtual presentation of hybrid collections made of originals and virtual replicas to boost attractiveness of an exhibition
- Physical replicas based on the 3D model of a cultural heritage artifact
- Loaning a high quality 3D virtual or physical replica as an alternative to loaning the original artifact (damage prevention, less or no insurance costs)
- Reusability of historically correct 3D models in documentaries, serious games or gaming and film industry
- Digital archive (digital preservation to prevent physical loss due to natural disasters)

The latter point in particular proves to be of high importance given the loss of priceless cultural heritage objects on various occasions connected with accidents or natural disasters, e.g. the fire at Herzogin Anna Amalia library in Weimar or the collapse of 30 shelf-kilometers of the Cologne historical archive in 2009 due to maintenance work on an underground subway line.

According to an extensive study (see Figure 1) of the Victoria and Albert Museum conducted in the framework of the Integrated Project 3D-COFORM[1], the 3D acquisition times of moderately sized objects (up to 50 by 50 by 50 cm) requires 5 to 20 hours with state-of-the-art structured light acquisition techniques for geometry and texture (colour) only – without considering view dependent reflectance properties. Structured light is considered the most appropriate technique for fine grained geometry acquisition of cultural resources in museums today. The acquisition times grow with the size and the complexity of the objects, if the geometric resolution constraint is not relaxed. A large share of the acquisition time is dedicated / required by manually repositioning the scanner, making the 3D digitization prohibitively expensive.

All in all, the process of building virtual surrogates from existing Cultural Heritage resources often requires an investment of several thousand EUROs per object. Given the fact that several hundreds of millions of objects exist in Cultural Heritage institutions (more than 130 million alone in the collection of the Smithsonian), these costs and time efforts are simply prohibitive.

---

[1] Website: http://3dcoform.eu – Last visited: 01.08.2013.

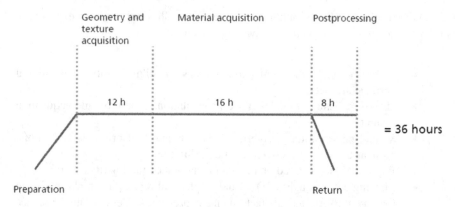

Fig. 2. Effort for 3D geometry, texture and material acquisition of bust-size objects

Given 120.000 new 3D artifact entries per year to the Berlin museums and one digitization device, this would mean that we need to achieve a digitization rate of 4.38 min per object. However, with current technology we estimate taking around 28 hours for the digitization alone and 36 hours including preparation, return and post-processing of the objects (see Figure 2). This leads to the situation that for 3D 'still no large scale practice' and 'no ordinary workflows' exist as Dr. Bienert of Staatliche Museen zu Berlin – Stiftung Preußischer Kulturbesitz (with more than 6 Mio. artifacts in their collection) points out in the Sector Advisory Board (SAB) of 3D-COFORM. That 3D acquisition is mainly a technology that is still 'used only sporadically for cherry-picked, selected objects'. This is also reflected by the current state of Europeana which - up to now - contains only a minimum amount of virtual 3D surrogates. However, the enormous potential of virtual 3D surrogates, their usefulness and benefits are undoubted for many applications in cultural institutions and beyond. This enormous potential will only be unlocked, if the following requirements are met: a) cost and time reduction, b) ease of use of 3D acquisition technology (minimize manual intervention), and c) develop and establish workflows. In addition, there is also the demand for developing acquisition and virtual presentation technology for classes of objects and materials which cannot be handled today.

2   Towards Economic Mass Digitization of 3D Artifacts

Cultural Heritage resources often show complex geometric properties (non-smooth surfaces, concavities, occlusions, etc.) and complicated optical materials (complex reflectance properties, translucent materials). One clear example is pieces in arts collections in museums - see the leftmost picture of Figure 3. Such Cultural Heritage items are made from materials with complex reflection properties, e.g. bronze, gold-plated, etc. For such materials, only prototypical acquisition techniques exist. These are not flexible with respect to object size and entail acquisition times in the order of many hours up to two working days. Moreover, there are considerable amounts of Cultural Heritage resources made from semi-transparent materials, e.g. jade, onyx, plastic, glass, tortoiseshell, marble, wax or crystal that show sub-surface scattering and translucency effects for which no practical acquisition technique yet exists. Capturing these properties faithfully is a key to creating suitable and useful virtual surrogates for many purposes, e.g. research, scholarship, exhibition planning, virtual exhibitions.

Fig. 3. Example objects from Victoria&Albert Museum (leftmost) and Staatliche Museen zu Berlin (two rightmost objects) showing different material properties

The common practice in Cultural Heritage is still the separate capture of geometry and reflectance. For the acquisition of 3D geometry many different approaches to this task, each with different focus, advantages and disadvantages, are known in the literature today [1]. Passive methods, such as multi-view stereo or depth from focus or shading, are capable of reconstructing a 3D scene from a pair or larger set of images taken under the natural illumination conditions. Common requirements are either strongly textured or ideal diffuse surfaces. However, these assumptions easily break down for many envisaged scenarios in cultural heritage, such as objects made from jade and typically the high resolution and accuracy of active techniques cannot be achieved [2]. In contrast, active techniques, such as laser-range-scanners or structured light approaches, directly emit light into the scene, either to provide correspondences for triangulation or to measure time-of-flight. Laser-based triangulation methods provide good depth-accuracy. However, the sequential nature of the measurement requires balancing resolution against measurement time. Additionally, the fact that laser-light is almost ideal monochromatic can pose a problem to the reconstruction of surfaces that do not ideally reflect light in the corresponding band of the spectrum.

With projector based structured light, one or more patterns that encode a bi-dimensional information are projected onto the object and images of that scene are captured with a camera. Due to the inherent parallelization (a projector can illuminate large portions of the object with a spatial pattern simultaneously and similarly the camera is capable of instantly capturing the complete covered area) structured light scans can be performed with considerable speed. One extreme example is the commercially successful Microsoft Kinect device that is capable of performing 30 scans per second based upon this principle, though at the price of a rather low quality. On the other hand, high-end scanners based on structured light provide a high accuracy down to 20μm [3]. Further, this technique has proven to be extremely robust with respect to complicated surface characteristics [4].

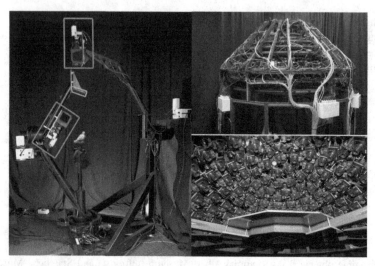

Fig. 4. Left: State of the Art setups for capturing geometry and reflectance of 3D objects: gonioreflectometer [5]; Right: DOME [6]

When considering the requirements of fast, versatile, and cost-efficient geometry and reflectance capture, it becomes apparent that none of the current state-of-the-art digitization setups is capable of satisfying all of them. There are basically two general approaches to the problem of capturing shape and reflectance of cultural resources with the desired quality: gonioreflectometers [5] or multiview domes [6] (see Figure 4). Their acquisition principle, consisting of capturing reflectance from many various light and view directions, is the same. Also, photographic cameras and synchronized light-sources are a common choice of hardware. Dome setups are limited by the fact that the necessary cameras and light sources are at fixed positions, at worst preventing the capture of certain regions of the object, possibly even depending on a disadvantageous placement of the object in the device. High frequency and angularly dependent material effects, such as very strong specular reflections, might also not be faithfully captured due to the fixed camera and light positions. Gonioreflectometers on the other hand rely on the principle of freely positioning one light-source and one camera. While these more flexible setups can capture much denser angular samplings, they are greatly restricted by acquisition time, rendering them virtually unusable for such an extensive measurement. Multiview domes on the other hand have a high degree of parallelism and hence comparably shorter capture times. However, both gonioreflectometers and the multiview domes still have other severe restrictions. Due to the rigid nature of the hardware, especially due to the fact that the camera operates at a fixed distance, the range of supported object sizes and fine-scale detail resolution is limited. Handling of concavities and self-occlusion is also impaired. The set of supported objects is therefore usually restricted to an extent of approximately 20cm x 20cm x 20cm and a "convex" shape without too many or deep holes.

From the above mentioned examples it becomes clear that not only does 3D digitization need to be fast and accurate, but also faithfully replicate optical material properties of the original cultural heritage artifacts.

We therefore identify a need for future research in the following areas:

- Much faster acquisition technology
  - o   Acquisition of optically complex objects
  - o   Acquisition of spatially varying materials
  - o   Acquisition of translucent / transparent materials
- Significant cost reduction of 3D digitization
- Ease of use
- Establishment and development of workflows for mass 3D digitization
- Knowledge transfer and guidelines
- More projects with critical mass
- Standardization of environmental conditions for comparable quality of scans

3   Towards Semantic Enrichment of Cultural Heritage Artifacts

In the real world our perception assists us in intuitively understanding and using existent information and knowledge, as well as the intrinsic relationships between the surrounding objects. The same level of cohesion between the available information and the digital representations of the physical world should be provided in the digital world.

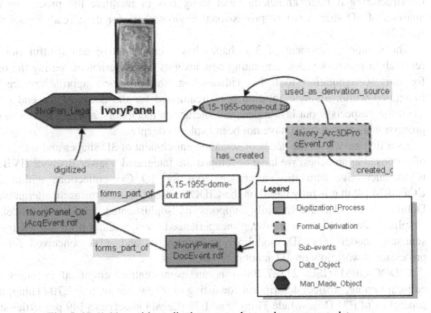

Fig. 5. 3D linking with media data, meta data and provenance data

For this purpose many different initiatives have tackled the challenges involved in the area of 3D annotations in the last 10 years, including projects such as AIM@SHAPE [7], Focus K3D [8], 3D-COFORM [9], V-MusT [10], Enhancing Engagement with 3D Heritage Data through Semantic Annotation [11], and Semantic Annotations for 3D Artifacts [12]. Current trends, like 3D Internet [13] or the Linking Open Data [14] movement, are also addressing these challenges. These initiatives have shown that the processes involved in annotating a digital 3D shape for semantic enrichment is complex and manifold. Although these and other projects have produced useful results, the technologies available to support 3D annotations do not offer a final solution. Thus, this remains an active area of research ([15], [16], [17], [18]), [19]), where different challenges need to be solved to fully support a semantic enrichment pipeline.

The digital representation (see Figure 5) of an artifact should consist of a geometric structure, accompanied by an annotation to associate semantics and context with its geometry or parts of its 3D shape. There are different techniques to understand the digital 3D shape ([20], [21]) and to formulate such geometric definitions ([16]), including sketching, painting, outlining, fitting, segmenting and structuring. On the semantic side there is much information and knowledge related to any 3D shape ([16]). The idea of representing semantically structured information and knowledge as well as creating links between the data has increasingly gained popularity, driven by the Semantic Web technologies [14]. Within the current research on annotations, most examples of structured information include semantic models for describing the intrinsic structure of the 3D shape ([22], [23], [24], [25]). Doerr and Theodoridou [26] proposed a model for describing the provenance (life-cycle) of digital 3D shapes in the Cultural Heritage domain ([27], [28], [29]). However, little attention has been paid on structuring domain knowledge and using this to facilitate the processing and analysis of 3D shapes within professional environments for the already established workflows.

The seantic enrichment of 3D shapes has been an active and fruitful field of research in previous years, generating new insights and experiences, setting the basis for our 3D-annotation tool. Notwithstanding, the proposed approaches are not integrated within a single solution nor streamlined for the needs of the end users. Therefore, aspects about layout designs, interaction metaphors, and workflows in real professional environments have not been explored deeply.

As a first answer to the needs of semantic enrichment of 3D shapes and integration of proposed approaches, we have developed the Integrated Viewer Browser (IVB). It is an interactive semantic enrichment tool for 3D CH collections within 3D-COFORM [9] that is fully based on the CIDOC-CRM [40] schema as an alternative to Dublin Core [41], and it fully supports its sophisticated annotation model. It simplifies user interaction, allowing inexperienced users, without prior knowledge on semantic models nor 3D modeling, to employ it, and it is conceived for the professional workflow on 3D annotation (see Figure 6).

CIDOC-CRM (ISO 21127:2006) is an event-centric, empirical ontology for cultural heritage artifact description consisting of 90 entities such as E70 (Thing) as a superclass of E71 (Man-Made Thing) and E72 (Legal Object) and 149 properties such as P43 (has dimension) or P101 (had general use) which can for example be attributed to E70 (Thing). Moreover our approach uses CRMdig, an extension to CIDOC-CRM for provenance documentation of artifacts to identify authors, locations, time, the content and the means used to create it. All metadata gathered is then encoded in RDF. Both, CIDOC-CRM and CRMdig help us generate a comprehensive documentation on cultural heritage artifacts. A more detailed discussion of the approach used can be found in [42] by our 3D-COFORM partners at TU-Graz and FORTH.

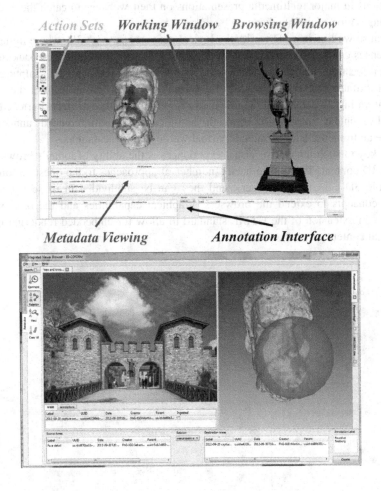

Fig. 6. General Graphical User Interface of our semantic enrichment tool, divided into 5 different sections – relation annotation between Maennerkopf bust and the Saalburg fort, represented by an image of its main entrance

4   3D Information Inside the Web

We notice an increasing interest in 3D for product presentation, visualization of abstract information (e.g. time lines) and for more intensive and enriching cultural heritage experiences.

Given the large number and variety of end-user devices, the world-wide-web has become the one connecting technology which allows device independent communication. Many cultural heritage institutions already embed flash videos and animations in major multimedia presentations on their websites to catch the attention and imagination of their audience.

Because we live in a 3D world, the logical next step is to go 3D, where immersive experiences can provide users with the ultimate sensation of being taken back in time to actual locations where they can marvel at architectural feats, artistic sculptures and ancient artifacts or even witness historic events unfolding right in front of their eyes. In addition highly detailed 3D digitization of cultural heritage artifacts enriched with valuable context information through geo-located, cross-referenced annotations provide an immense add-on value to virtual web-based presentations.

The key to such innovative visual experiences is the ability of today's browsers to render 3D content. There have been a number of approaches to the question, on how to enable 3D content in browsers, and they can be subdivided in those which use plugin concepts to extend the browsers' graphical capabilities and the ones which propose an extension of the HTML standard to allow for embedded rendering of 3D graphical content.

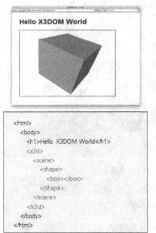

```
40   webGLProgramObject = gl.createProgram();
41
42   // Der folgende String enthaelt den kompletten Quellcode
43   // fuer einen minimalistischen Vertex-Shader:
44   vShaderQuellcode =
45        'attribute vec4 vPosition; \n\
46        void main() \n\
47        { \n\
48            gl_Position = vPosition; \n\
49        } \n';
50   // Das Vertex-Shader-Objekt wird angelegt:
51   vShader = gl.createShader(gl.VERTEX_SHADER);
52   // - mit seinem Quelltext verknuepft:
53   gl.shaderSource(vShader, vShaderQuellcode);
54   // - kompiliert:
55   gl.compileShader(vShader);
56   // - dem Shader-Program-Objekt hinzugefuegt:
57   gl.attachShader(webGLProgramObject, vShader);
58
```

Fig. 7. X3DOM and WebGL

Currently there are lots of free or commercial third party browser tools or plugins available. [30, 31, 32] have produced a comprehensive list of 3D web-technology, including plugin technology (e.g. X3D, Java3D, Flash) and plugin-less technologies like Canvas3D and 3D on 2D-pipeline systems using SVG and canvas rendering. As a successor to CANVAS3D [33], the WebGL API is embedded into JavaScript originally designed to create dynamic web pages.

The final specification of WebGL has been published in [34]. A number of middleware components already make use of this low-level API [35, 36, 37] to extend their functionality. WebGL defines a rendering context for graphical content within HTML5 on top of which X3D using the HTML DOM is placed.

X3DOM is declarative X3D in HTML5 (see Figure 7). It allows utilizing well-known JavaScript and DOM infrastructure for 3D and brings together both:

- Declarative content design as known from web design
- "old school" imperative approaches known from game engine development

The advantage of using X3DOM is seamless integration of 3D content in web browsers.

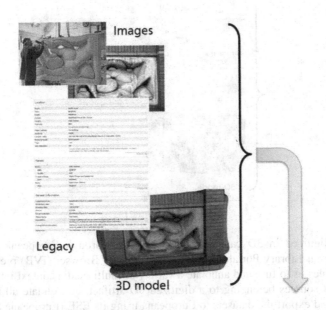

Fig. 8. Annotating 3D artifacts with IVB and export to Europeana

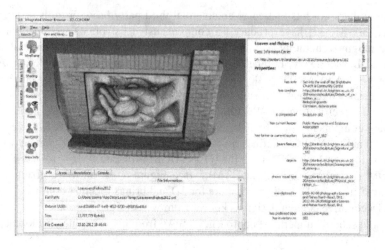

3D-COFORM
Integrated Viewer Browser (IVB)

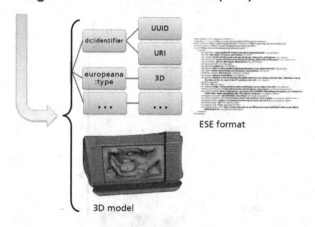

Fig. 8. (*Continued*)

Artifacts digitized in 3D can already be accessed through Europeana [38], the European Digital Library Portal. The Integrated Viewer Browser (IVB) presented in section 3 enables us to fuse and annotate a variety of multi-media context information from different sources belonging to a digitized 3D artifact, consolidate all pieces of information and export the datasets to Europeana using its ESE (Europeana Semantic Elements) [39] metadata format, a Dublin Core-based set of fields with 12 additional specific Europeana elements to display records appropriately.

Compared to CARARE [43], we simplify the acquisition of meta-data from users and produce arbitrary output formats. However, Carare also contributes with 3D virtual content to Europeana through tools that convert exisiting metadata to the Carara intermediate format from which it is converted to Europeana ESE metadata format.

Fig. 9. Data record in Europeana and link to interactive 3D presentation in browser

5   Conclusion

In this paper we have motivated why there is a need for economic 3D mass digitization technologies and presented its challenges. We have also established the requirements for an integrated approach defining an ontology for the cultural heritage domain to semantically enrich digitized artifacts with media data, meta data and provenance data based on standards such as CIDOC-CRM. We have demonstrated the annotation of 3D objects consolidating multi-media context information from a variety of sources, as well as export to Europeana and integrated, interactive 3D visualization of data records in regular web browsers.

The overall goal of our efforts is to develop a consolidated solution that integrates fast and economic 3D mass digitization technologies with our IVB and our decentralized CIDOC-CRM-based distributed database for identification, classification, annotation and storage of cultural heritage artifacts using cloud services and which is located in museum depots to digitize all new entries. Alternatively a system like that should be rented for a limited period of time from licensed service providers making digitization affordable for small and medium size museums as well. We expect the costs for digitization of individual artifacts to drop by a magnitude at least due to the increased throughput, while preserving the same high quality accuracy of the geometry, texture and material property acquisition process as with prior more manual approaches.

We envisage future challenges and potential technical solutions in the following fields:

- Automation of 3D digitization and annotation
- Internet 3D search engines (shape retrieval)
- Combined search capabilities by
  - Meta data: from integrated heterogeneous meta data sources
  - Shape: Sketch-based retrieval combined with expectation lists
  - Materials: search using ground-truth data
- Organizational challenges such as
  - Rights management: access, use, distribution
  - Certification of provenance: COAs for 3D models by certified institutions

It is our belief that 3D Internet, supported by technologies such as WebGl, X3D and HTML5, can tremendously benefit the creation and accessibility of virtual 3D cultural heritage artifacts. While there are still some persisting challenges concerning economic 3D data acquisition and organization, future synergies combining cloud computing and mobile devices with linked open data, might help to overcome them.

References

[1] Sansoni, G., Trebeschi, M., Docchio, F.: State-of -the-Art and Applications of 3D Imaging Sensors in Industry, Cultural Heritage, Medicine, and Criminal Investigation. Sensors 9(1), 568–601 (2009)

[2] Seitz, S., Curless, B., Diebel, J., Scharstein, D., Szeliski, R.: A Comparison and Evaluation of Multi-View Stereo Reconstruction Algorithms. In: Conference on Computer Vision and Pattern Recognition, vol. 1, pp. 519–526 (2006)

[3] Ritz, M., Langguth, F., Scholz, M., Goesele, M., Stork, A.: High resolution acquisition of detailed surfaces with lens-shifted structured light. Computers & Graphics 36(1), 16–27 (2012)

[4] Gupta, M., Agrawal, A., Veeraraghavan, A., Narasimhan, S.G.: Structured Light 3D Scanning in the presence of Global Illumination. In: Proceedings of the CVPR 2011, pp. 713–720 (2011)

[5] Holroyd, M., Lawrence, J., Zickler, T.: A coaxial optical scanner for synchronous acquisition of 3D geometry and surface reflectance. SIGGRAPH, Article 99, 12 pages (2010)

[6] Schwartz, C., Weinmann, M., Ruiters, R., Klein, R.: Integrated High-Quality Acquisition of Geometry and Appearance for Cultural Heritage. In: The 12th International Symposium on Virtual Reality, Archeology and Cultural Heritage, VAST 2011, pp. 25–32 (2011)

[7] Project: AIM@SHAPE, http://www.aimatshape.net/ (last visited: February 12, 2013)

[8] Project: FOCUS K3D, http://www.focusk3d.eu/ (last visited: February 02, 2013)

[9] Project: 3D-COFORM, http://www.3d-coform.eu (last visited: February 12, 2013)

[10] Project V-MusT, http://www.v-must.net/ (last visited: February 12, 2013)

[11] Project: Enhancing engagement with 3D heritage data through semantic annotation, http://www.ddsgsa.net/projects/empire/Empire/Home.html   (last visited: February 12, 2013)

[12] Semantic annotations for 3D artefacts project, http://itee.uq.edu.au/~eresearch/projects/3dsa   (last   visited: February 12, 2013)

[13] Alpcan, T., Bauckhage, C., Kotsovinos, E.: Towards 3d internet: Why, what, and how? In: Proceedings of the International Conference on Cyberworlds, CW 2007, pp. 95–99 (October 2007)

[14] Linking open data, http://esw.w3.org/SweoIG/TaskForces/CommunityProjects/LinkingOpenData (last visited: December 02, 2013)

[15] Havemann, S., Fellner, D.W.: Seven research challenges of generalized 3D documents. IEEE Comput. Graph.Appl. 27(3), 70–76 (2007)

[16] Spagnuolo M., Falcidieno B.: 3D media and the semantic web. IEEE Intelligent Systems, 90–96 (March/April 2009)

[17] Torsten, U., Settgast, V., Berndt, R.: Semantic enrichment for 3D documents techniques and open problems. In: ELPUB: 14th International Conference on Electronic Publishing: Publishing in the Networked World: Transforming the Nature of Communication, Helsinki, Finland, pp. 374–384 (2010)

[18] Koller, D., Frischer, B., Humphreys, G.: Research challenges for digital archives of 3D cultural heritage models. Journal of Computing and Cultural Heritage 2(3), 1–17 (2010)

[19] Catalano, C., Mortara, M., Spagnuolo, M., Falcidieno, B.: Semantics and 3D media: Current issues and perspectives. Computers & Graphics 35(4), 869–877 (2011)

[20] Attene, M., Biasotti, S., Mortara, M., Patané, G., Spagnuolo, M., Falcidieno, B.: Computational methods for understanding 3D shapes. Computers & Graphics 30(3), 323–333 (2006)

[21] De Floriani, L., Magillo, P., Papaleo, L., Puppo, E.: Shape modeling and understanding: Research trends and results of the G3 group at DISI

[22] Floriani, L.D., Papaleo, L., Carissimi, N.: A Java3D framework for inspecting and segmenting 3D models. In: Proceedings of the 13th International Symposium on 3D Web Technology, Los Angeles, California, pp. 67–74. ACM (2008)

[23] Papaleo, L., De Floriani, L.: Semantic-based segmentation and annotation of 3D models. In: Foggia, P., Sansone, C., Vento, M. (eds.) ICIAP 2009. LNCS, vol. 5716, pp. 103–112. Springer, Heidelberg (2009)

[24] Attene, M., Robbiano, F., Patané, G., Mortara, M., Spagnuolo, M., Falcidieno, B.: Semantic annotation of digital 3D objects. In: Albertoni, R., Mortara, M. (eds.) SAMT (Posters and Demos), vol. 300. CEUR-WS.org (2007)

[25] Attene, M., Robbiano, F., Spagnuolo, M., Falcidieno, B.: Part-Based annotation of virtual 3D shapes. In: Proceedings of the 2007 International Conference on Cyberworlds, pp. 427–436. IEEE Computer Society (2007)

[26] Doerr, M., Theodoriou, M.: CRMdig: a generic digital provenance model for scientific observation. In: Proceedings of 3rd USENIX Workshop on the Theory and Practice of Provenance, Heraklion, Crete, Greece (2011)

[27] Rodriguez Echavarria, K., Morris, D., Arnold, D.: Web based presentation of semantically tagged 3D content for public sculptures and monuments in the UK. In: Proceedings of the 14th International Conference on 3D Web Technology, Darmstadt, Germany, pp. 119–126. ACM (2009)

[28] Havemann, S., Settgast, V., Berndt, R., Eide, O., Fellner, D.W.: The arrigo showcase reloaded - towards a sustainable link between 3D and semantics. J. Comput. Cult. Herit. 2(1), 1–13 (2009)

[29] Pena Serna, S., Scopigno, R., Doerr, M., Theodoriou, M., Georgis, C., Ponchio, F., Stork, A.: 3D-centered media linking and semantic enrichment through integrated searching, browsing, viewing and annotating. In: VAST 2011: The 12th International Symposium on Virtual Reality, Archaeology and Intelligent Cultural Heritage, Prato, Italy (2011)

[30] Behr, J., Eschler, P., Jung, Y., Zoellner, P.M.: X3DOM – a DOM-based HTML5/ X3D integration model. In: Proceedings Web3D 2009, pp. 127–135. ACM Press, New York (2009)

[31] Behr, J., Jung, Y., Keil, J., Drevensek, T., Eschler, P., Zoellner, M., Fellner, D.: A scalable architecture for the HTML5/ X3D integration model X3DOM. In: Proc. Web3D, pp. 185–193. ACM Press, New York (2010)

[32] Behr, J., Jung, Y., Drevensek, T., Aderhold, A.: Dynamic and interactive aspects of X3DOM. In: Proceedings of the 16th International Conference on 3D Web Technology (Web3D 2011), pp. 81–87. ACM, New York (2011),
http://doi.acm.org/10.1145/2010425.2010440,
doi:10.1145/2010425.2010440

[33] Vukicevic, V.: Canvas 3d (2009),
http://blog.vlad1.com/2007/11/26/canvas-3d-gl-power-web-style/ (last visited: February 12, 2013)

[34] Webgl specification,
https://cvs.khronos.org/svn/repos/registry/trunk/public/webgl/doc/spec/WebGL-spec.html (last visited: December 02, 2013)

[35] Kay, L.: Scenejs (2010), http://www.scenejs.org/ (last visited: February 12, 2013)
[36] Brunt, P.: Glge (2010), http://www.glge.org/ (last visited: February 12, 2013)
[37] Benedetto, M.D., Ponchio, F., Ganovelli, F., Scopigno, R.: Spidergl: a javascript 3d graphics library for next-generation www. In: Proc. Web3D 2010, pp. 165–174. ACM, New York (2010)
[38] Project: Europeana, http://www.europeana.eu (last visited: February 12, 2013)
[39] ESE Europeana metadata format, http://www.europeana.eu/schemas/ese/ (last visited: February 12, 2013)
[40] Crofts, N., Doerr, M., Gill, T., Stead, S., Stiff, M.: Definition of the CIDOC Conceptual Reference Model, ISO (2005)
[41] Dublin Core Metadata Initiative (DCMI), Dublin Core, http://dublincore.org
[42] Schröttner, M., Havemann, S., Theodoridou, M., Doerr, M., Fellner, D.W.: A generic approach for generating cultural heritage metadata. In: Ioannides, M., Fritsch, D., Leissner, J., Davies, R., Remondino, F., Caffo, R. (eds.) EuroMed 2012. LNCS, vol. 7616, pp. 231–240. Springer, Heidelberg (2012)
[43] Hansen, H.J., Fernie, K.: CARARE: Connecting archaeology and architecture in europeana. In: Ioannides, M., Fellner, D., Georgopoulos, A., Hadjimitsis, D.G. (eds.) EuroMed 2010. LNCS, vol. 6436, pp. 450–462. Springer, Heidelberg (2010)

Web and Mobile Visualization for Cultural Heritage

Marco Di Benedetto, Federico Ponchio, Luigi Malomo, Marco Callieri,
Matteo Dellepiane, Paolo Cignoni, and Roberto Scopigno

Visual Computing Lab, CNR-ISTI, via Moruzzi 1, 56124 Pisa, Italy
{marco.dibenedetto,federico.ponchio,luigi.malomo,
marco.callieri,matteo.dellepiane,paolo.cignoni,
roberto.scopigno}@isti.cnr.it

Abstract. Thanks to the impressive research results produced in the last decade,
digital technologies are now mature for producing high-quality digital replicas
of Cultural Heritage (CH) artifacts. At the same time, CH practitioners and
scholars have also access to a number of technologies that allow distributing
and presenting those models to everybody and everywhere by means of a
number of communication platforms. The goal of this chapter is to present some
recent technologies for supporting the visualization of complex models, by
focusing on the requirements of interactive manipulation and visualization of
3D models on the web and on mobile platforms. The section will present some
recent experiences where high-quality 3D models have been used in CH
research, restoration and conservation. Some open issues in this domain will
also be presented and discussed.

Keywords: Web-based graphics, digital 3D models, mobile platforms,
interactive visualization and navigation.

1 Introduction

The progress in optical systems and visual computing has produced a number of
mature technologies for producing high-quality digital 3D replicas of Cultural
Heritage (CH) artifacts. Given the progressive availability of accurate and information
dense digital 3D models, the web and the mobile devices are ideal platforms for the
dissemination of those cultural assets.

Given the availability of technologies able to produce *high-resolution models* (with
high-resolution we mean sampled models counting from 5M up to hundreds of
millions faces/points) that are also characterized by high-quality mapping of the color
or reflection properties [1, 2, 3], the issues are now: how to encode efficiently those
data; how to archive and make them accessible to the community; and how to
visualize them efficiently in the framework of CH applications [4].

Many approaches for supporting *interactive visualization* of complex models have
been presented in the last ten years; our goal in this work is to focus on the
technologies that allow implementing interactive manipulation and visualization of
3D models on the web and on mobile platforms. Many view-dependent rendering

M. Ioannides and E. Quak (Eds.): 3D Research Challenges, LNCS 8355, pp. 18–35, 2014.

solutions have been presented, able to process a multi-resolution model and extracting frame-by-frame view-dependent representations that fulfill the rendering quality and the performance constraints. Some of these solutions are now available on the entire spectrum of platforms (from desktop computers to tablets and smartphones, linked to the internet by wire or by mobile wireless connection), demonstrating that we dispose of a common enabling technology able to carry high-quality graphics to everyone and everywhere. Section 2 will focus on this theme.

Human-computer interaction is another major issue, specifically when the focus is a domain where users are usually not ICT professionals. If we focus on CH applications, then the potential users are museum visitors, CH curators, restorers, scholars; therefore, we cannot assume that the average skill in manipulating digital 3D objects or scenes will be the one we experience in the gaming domain or in any other domain where fluency with Computer Graphics interaction technique is a prerequisite skill. Interaction with 3D objects or scenes usually is not a simple task, due to the not uniform management approaches used by different systems and the risk of losing yourself in the void space while manipulating or navigating a virtual scene. Section 3 presents a new approach to the virtual manipulation of an object and for the interactive selection of view. We illustrate the results of an implementation of a navigation paradigm over a mobile platform that supports multi-touch interaction (incorporated in the "MeshLab for iOS" application, http://www.meshpad.org/). A number of preliminary evaluations, carried out with test subjects, and the feedback received from real users from different CH fields demonstrated that the multi-touch approach is much easier to use than the traditional mouse-based trackball. The result has been an impressively short time required to learn how to drive the interactive navigation around an object, including zooming and panning.

Integration of different media described in in Section 4 is the last issue that will be discussed. Virtual 3D models are just one of the available media that are used to document the status and the beauty of our CH assets. Images (both the standard ones and the more advanced 2D media such as RTI or panoramic images) play an important role; video is a resource easier and easier to acquire and to distribute to users. The improved insight that can be gathered by the use of multiple media should be taken into account, preventing CG people from stressing only the use of the 3D media. This means designing and developing technologies able to link different media or to present them in a coordinated or integrated manner. Several interesting approaches have been presented recently: web systems which allow to present and inspect 2D and 3D representations (e.g. the Cenobium system, http://cenobium.isti.cnr.it/ [5]; visualization tools that allow to inspect and analyze different types of images and 3D data (e.g. the YALE open source visualization system [6]); and systems able to navigate interactively a 3D scene and a set of geo-located 2D images (e.g. the PhotoCloud system, http://vcg.isti.cnr.it/photocloud/). Finally, another major advance would be also to create a more tight and coherent relation between any *digital model* and the *text* that encodes our knowledge on the story and meaning of the represented artwork. We will present some preliminary results on the design of a system able to support links from the text to the 3D object and vice-versa, providing therefore an unprecedented tight integration between these two media.

2   Interactive Rendering of Complex Models

The quality of current 3D sampling methodologies makes the reconstruction of high-resolution digital models of the artworks of interest an off-the-shelf capability. Standard short-range acquisition devices allow to produce at least 4-10 samples for squared millimeter, thus leading to digital models composed by several millions or tens of millions sampled points. Long range technologies support coarser sampling densities per squared unit, but since the sampled surface extension is usually much larger, models with up to hundreds of million samples are also common. Even Multi-view stereo techniques are now able to handle thousands of images, and provide extremely dense 3D models.

The value of the models reconstructed with modern sampling technologies resides in their accuracy and density, meaning that we have a huge quantity of geometric data to be used in applications. But, at the same time, all those data can be a problem for implementing efficient computations or visualization; a very common concern raised very often in the near past was that the density of sampled models made it impossible to use them in real applications. Therefore, endorsing methods able to produce a controlled granularity reduction of the digital models is mandatory in CH applications.

2.1   Simplification and Multiresolution Management of Complex Models

Many years of research in computer graphics have been instrumental in building an arsenal of technologies for controlled surface simplification and for the construction of multiresolution encoding schemes and view-dependent rendering modalities [7, 8]. The work at CNR-ISTI led to the design of several approaches and tools that contributed to this evolution. Most of them have been distributed to the community. Efficient tools for the simplification of triangulated surfaces are nowadays supported in MeshLab (http://meshlab.sourceforge.net/) and are also at the base of a multiresolution representation and rendering library, called *Nexus* (http://vcg.isti.cnr.it/nexus/).

Nexus is a multiresolution visualization library supporting interactive rendering of very large surface models. It belongs to the family of cluster based, view-dependent visualization algorithms (see for example the Adaptive Tetrapuzzles [9] and the Batched Multi Triangulation (BMT) [10] approaches). It employs a *patch-based approach*: the granularity of the primitive elements is moved from triangles to small contiguous portions of a mesh (patches composed by a few thousand triangles), to reduce the number of per-element CPU operations. Moreover, a batched structure allows for aggressive GPU optimization of the triangle patches; the latter are usually encoded with triangle strips, boosting GPU rendering performances.

To hold and manage the large number of alternative patches that compose the multiresolution encoding, Nexus adopts a spatial partitioning strategy based on KD-trees, which combines fast streaming construction of the multiresolution model with efficient adaptive spatial partitioning of the mesh.

Fig. 1. An example of view dependent rendering by means of the Nexus library: the images on the top show different frames of a zooming-in navigation (moving towards a selected region of the surface) over the 3D model of the Portalada of Ripoll (Spain); the images below show the subdivision in patches of the view-dependent representations used to produce the images above

The Nexus multiresolution encoding is built from a triangle soup (or a point-based representation), by following iteratively the steps below:

1. The triangles from the triangle soup stream are inserted into a space subdivision structure (based on a KD-tree);
2. For each leaf of the KD-tree the triangles are collected, and a small mesh is generated and saved as a node in the multiresolution model;
3. The borders of the mesh (the triangles whose vertices do not fully belong to the node) are marked as read-only and the mesh is simplified using a high quality quadric-error simplification algorithm, leaving the patch borders unchanged;
4. Finally the triangles of the simplified mesh are pushed (and shuffled) into a new triangle soup stream, and the procedure is applied from the beginning again.

After each iteration, the number of triangles is halved and a new set of potential derivation between corresponding set of patches is constructed. These possible rules for replacement of patches are stored in a directed acyclic graph (DAG) and used at rendering time to produce the view-dependent representation.

Rendering a Nexus model requires a traversal of this DAG, to select an appropriate cut and the corresponding set of patches that will produce the view-dependent representation extracted from the current frame (see Figure 1). For each node we estimate the screen space error using a bounding sphere and the simplification error recorded during the construction stage. Only the DAG has to be kept in RAM during the selection of each view-dependent representation. This means that a small memory size is needed to store the multiresolution structure. The data corresponding to the selected patches are loaded from disk on demand. This results in a very low number of OpenGL function calls (on the order of one thousand) even for large models and this allows to obtain efficient rendering performances.

The Nexus scheme supports the management of models with attached color data. The current Nexus version supports meshes adopting the *color-per-vertex* approach (this is common for very dense meshes, where the color per vertex encoding is more efficient than texture mapping). We are extending Nexus to support also triangle meshes having the color channel mapped by textures.

2.2   Complex Models on the Web

The web is now perceived as the main channel for accessing information through a wide variety of multimedia representations, and for managing the documentation of a CH artwork. Enabling technologies are therefore required to support easy access to multimedia representations on the web and high-quality visualization directly inside standard web pages. The delivery of 3D content through the web comes with a considerable delay with respect to other digital media such as text, still images, videos and sound. Just like it already happened for commodity platforms, 3D content visualization is the latest of the functionalities acquired by web browsers.

Originally, 3D content was used only locally; nevertheless, remote visualization was perceived as an important feature, and thus collaborative and remote rendering solutions were proposed since the '90s. Then, several different approaches have been proposed for distributing and visualizing 3D data on the web (e.g. VRLM, X3D); the disadvantage of those approaches was that they confined 3D data to a specific visualization tool, implemented as a plugin (i.e., binary executable modules external to the hosting browser) that had to be explicitly installed by users. This approach was not ideal for the CH community, where potential users are usually not ICT experts and where the appearance of a blank screen corresponding to a request of installation of a piece of software frequently discourages the user from further exploration.

Fortunately, the evolution of the web is helping us. The appearance of the WebGL standard in 2009 [11] was a fundamental change. WebGL is the newborn component of the OpenGL ecosystem, and it is modeled as a JavaScript Application Programming Interface (API) that exposes a one-to-one mapping to the OpenGL ES 2.0 specifications. WebGL provides therefore a specification on how to render 3D data, that web browsers should implement. Hence, by incorporating the WebGL approach, modern web browsers are able to natively access the 3D graphics hardware without needing additional plug-ins or extensions. Since WebGL is a low-level API, a series of higher-level libraries have been developed to help both expert and non-expert users in the design and implementation of applications. They differ from each other by the programming paradigm they use, ranging from scene-graph-based interfaces, such as X3Dom [12], to procedural paradigms, like SpiderGL [13].

WebGL has been already used to implement complex rendering systems and different interaction modalities in several fields.

There is an enormous potential brought by WebGL for CH applications development. This is not just because we do not need anymore to install specific plugins, but also because WebGL allows 3D data to become one of the media that can be shown in a web page natively. We are no more confining digital 3D assets to the ghetto of the specific plugin, but we are immersing them in the full multimedia context.

The easy visualization of 3D models is an immediate result that can be produced with browsers that endorse WebGL. Some examples in the CH domain are the access to a repository of 3D models produced by Fraunhofer IGD in the framework of the 3DCOFORM project (see at http://www.3d-coform.eu/x3dom/index.html) or the recent re-design of the Cenobium system (see at http://cenobium.isti.cnr.it/ or Figure 2).

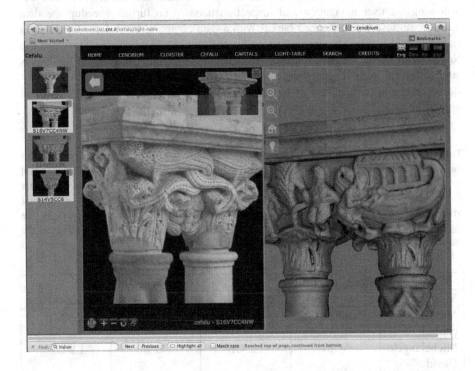

Fig. 2. An example of visual presentation provided by the Cenobium system [5]: in the same window we have a side by side visualization of a high-resolution image (left), and of a 3D model (right) of two different capitols from the Cefalù cloister (Sicily, Italy)

CH applications are very often based on complex 3D models: therefore, efficient transmission and visualization of 3D models becomes immediately an issue.

To efficiently render large 3D models on the web, we ported our Nexus approach to WebGL. The view-dependent rendering engine of the Nexus system has been ported from C++ to JavaScript on top of SpiderGL, revealing that JavaScript performances were not a limit due to the minimal processing required by the Nexus library (a simple traversal of the multiresolution hierarchy); the limitations of WebGL with respect to the more complex desktop OpenGL API were also not a problem due to the very basic OpenGL features required by Nexus. Obviously, using a multiresolution encoding introduces some penalty in terms of storage, since the multiresolution encoding is usually larger in size than the input mesh. We report in Table 1 some figures on the triangle meshes presented in this paper. To support fast data transfer we adopted a streaming approach over HTTP; Nexus objects are stored on a standard hard disk on our web server and served directly by any HTTP server (we used the Apache server). Being based on a multiresolution approach, the Nexus rendering engine sends data to the remote client on demand, i.e. low resolution data is transferred at the beginning of the visualization session and only the required details are transferred later on, following the user navigation and inspection needs. To further speedup the data transfer we have also enhanced Nexus with a data compression feature; the 3D data encoding tool is now able to perform geometric and topologic compression over the Nexus triangle patches. Unfortunately, this technology cannot be used in the Nexus porting for the WebGL platform, since the Javascript implementation of the client-side decompression stage is way too slow and degrades the performances, rather than improving them.

Table 1. Some figures on a few dataset (most of them shown in the paper figures): size of the input mesh and size of the Nexus encoding (without compression). Monreale capitol is one sample capitol presented in the Cenobium system, Monreale Cloister (http://cenobium.isti.cnr.it/). Michelangelo David is the model produced by the Digital Michelangelo project (https://graphics.stanford.edu/projects/mich/). Ruthwell Cross is the digital model of an 8th cent. Anglo-Saxon cross in UK. Finally, the Ripoll Portalada is the model of a large and carved church portal in Ripoll, Catalona, Spain.

	Plain input mesh		Nexus encoding	
Model	No. faces	Space (MB)	No. faces	Space (MB)
Monreale capitol	4.8 M	96 MB	9.5 M	159 MB
Michelangelo David	56 M	1.2 GB	112 M	1.9 GB
Ruthwell Cross	112 M	2.5 GB	224 M	3.7 GB
Ripoll Portalada	178 M	3.6 GB	354 M	5.8 GB

Nexus is the technology used to support most of our current projects deploying 3D on the web (e.g. the Cenobium system [5]). A recent result of the EC "3DCOFORM" project (http://www.3d-coform.eu/) was the Community Presenter (http://vcg.isti.cnr.it/presenter/). Community Presenter is a collection of tools and templates for the creation of multimedia interactive presentations of cultural artifacts, represented by means of their digital 3D model. The target audience is CH personnel (an art historian or a museum staff member with limited ICT experience or just assisted by an ICT professional). The Community Presenter allows easy visualization in HTML pages or QML applications of media such as 3D models, images, Reflection Transformation Images (RTI), video and audio. As a main feature, it supports the streaming of multiresolution 3D meshes over HTTP (using the previously discussed Nexus format), allowing the exploration of very large models. The code is based on declarative programming and extensive use of templates: this allows basic users to build presentation by simply filling in a few variable values (names of models, settings etc.) and without preventing advanced users from modifying interfaces and adding advanced functionalities. Community Presenter has already been used to design some informative systems, which were part of the assessment and dissemination actions of the 3DCOFORM projects. Some of these have been shown in the temporary exhibition that took place in Brighton on July-August 2012 (http://www.3d-coform.eu/index.php/dissemination/exhibitions).

One of these preliminary results is a multimedia kiosk that tells the story of a set of coins from the collection of the San Matteo National Museum (Pisa, Italy). Coins are an ideal test bed to show the potential of multimedia systems, since they are very small artworks and in a standard museum exposition they are presented to the public from a distance (typically at least 50cm from the observer's eye). This distance does not allow visitors to note the small and interesting details on the legend or on the carved decoration of the coins; moreover, coins are usually visible only from one side. Furthermore, coins have a lot of hidden knowledge that is difficult to transfer to visitors in an easy, effective and understandable manner. Therefore, the Community Presenter tool has been used to present those ancient coins in an innovative way [14], to better capture the interest of visitors and to give them enhanced information (see Figure 3). In the case of this multimedia presentation, we decided to use an advanced 2D image-based representation rather than a standard 3D medium. The requirement was to support the easy manipulation of the coins and the dynamic change of illumination, in order to allow the users to inspect those small artifacts in detail. This means that we needed a virtual representation capable of simulating illumination effects in real-time and in an accurate way, producing photo-realistic renderings. Therefore, to support easy and high-quality relighting of the digital coins, we decided to digitize them by acquiring RTI. RTI encoding is a computational photography method that, starting from a set of images taken from a single view under varying lighting conditions, encodes the object surface reflection (apparent color) by means of a function of the incident light direction. This encoding enables the interactive relighting of the object from any direction. A few snapshots from the coin multimedia kiosk are presented in Figure 3.

The results obtained with this installation let us broaden the practical use of in-browser 3D hardware acceleration: apart from efficiently using WebGL for 3D scenery visualization, we were able to exploit the power of the underlying graphics system to provide useful and complex effects even on 2D data (e.g. images), enabling a performance-oriented and cooperative interaction between Computer Vision and Computer Graphics methodologies.

Obviously, being able to include 3D data in web pages and supporting interactive rendering is not enough. Our skill and focus is on 3D interactive visualization, hence the content and focus of this section. But we would like to state explicitly here that the availability of 3D data on the web is a poor and incomplete result if a correct and complete management of the associated metadata is not supported and made accessible. The 3D model should therefore be paired by data that clarify *what* is the CH artwork represented and *how* the digital model was created (qualification of the digital model creation process). The absence or presence of these data makes the distinctions between a nice model and a trustable/usable digital document. We direct the interested readers to the many papers appeared in the last few years on the issues on metadata creation, management and searching [23,24] in the context of 3D data for the cultural heritage domain.

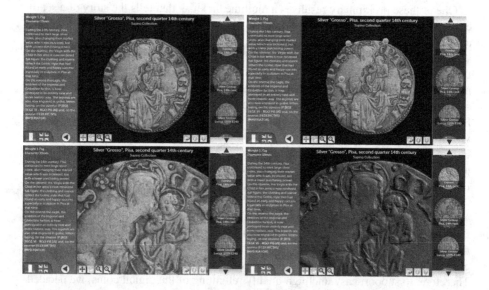

Fig. 3. Four snapshots taken from the multimedia kiosk of the San Matteo Museum (Pisa, Italy), showing different visualizations features provided by the coin viewer, like links to more detailed information (top right), navigation on high resolution images (bottom left) and interactive relighting (bottom right)

2.3   Porting 3D to the Mobile Platforms

Given the impressive technological evolution of the mobile platforms (smartphones and tablets) and their enormous commercial success, many applications are migrating towards the mobile domain. Transmission and rendering of 3D models is possible also on these platforms, but the specificity of both the delivery channel and the presentation platform opens some issues. Some of those issues are common to the web-based domain: efficient transmission of complex data should be ensured (mobile systems have stronger limitation on bandwidth than standard internet connections); efficient and interactive rendering should be supported, even on complex models (and thus multiresolution is required to sustain interactive rendering rates on complex models). Another issue specifically raised by the mobile platform is the need for efficient and easy-to-use manipulation interfaces (see the next section for a brief discussion of this issue).

Smartphones or tablets could become very effective devices to present visual data. In the specific CH domain, this is definitely the case of the systems supporting the visitors of museums or of historical cities (several interactive virtual guides have been developed and experimented with recently based on portable devices). Another application could be assisting restorers in the annotation of the status of an artwork, or in the documentation of a restoration work. These portable devices could be the ideal platform for supporting the inspection and the annotation process (on top of digital representations that can be either 2D images or 3D models).

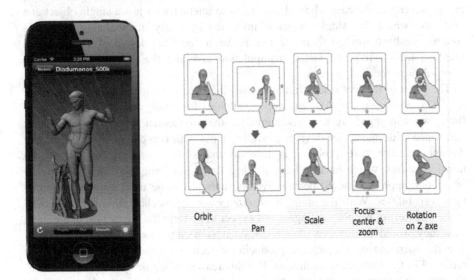

Fig. 4. MeshLab on iOS (on the left) and the touch-based interaction adopted to manipulate the virtual object

A corresponding research project was started at CNR-ISTI at the end of 2011, aimed at developing a visualizer for 3D meshes that should run on smartphones or tablets. We planned to move to those platforms just the visualization component of MeshLab. This tool has been released for both the Apple iOS (http://www.meshpad.org/) and the Android (https://play.google.com/store/apps/details?id=it.isticnr.meshlab) platforms. The goal was to implement a viewer for 3D models (single objects, rather than complex architectures). The viewer reads a variety of file formats and supports interactive rendering of meshes of size up to 1M - 2M faces. For a more efficient rendering of larger models, we recently ported the Nexus approach also on this platform (the corresponding update for the app will be released in the third quarter of 2013).

3   Manipulation and Interaction

Interaction with CH models is a very complex task, since this specific application domain requires several different access modalities and presents some associated open issues [15], since we need new approaches to support: efficient and easy *manipulation* and *visual inspection* (single object in focus) [16]; efficient and easy *navigation* of large scenes (e.g. architectures) [17]; finally, we should design and experiment with *natural* or *disappearing interfaces* (gesture-based, tracking via Kinect-like devices, etc.).

So far we have been focusing mostly on the first class of interaction techniques, giving priority to the case where the user has to interact with just a single object at a time, and where this single object is inspected by freely manipulating it. In this context, we have worked so far on two research lines: the design of a multi-touch interface for this type of visual manipulation task and the design of constrained manipulations for 3D browsers.

The result of the first research line was the interface implemented for the *MeshLab for iOS* tool (Figure 4), an app available for free on the Apple Store (http://www.meshpad.org/). Conventionally, the manipulation-style interaction is performed with interaction devices providing input with two degree of freedom, like the mouse. The core problem is how to map this limited interaction to 3D transformations, which have at least six degrees of freedom. More importantly, the interaction approach should be intuitive and natural for the user, even with limited input capabilities. With the *multi-touch interaction* approaches provided on current mobile platforms, people use fingers and expect to perform the interaction in the same way they would do for everyday tasks. That is because touch technology allows directly operating on the screen, producing a feeling of naturalness that must be reflected in the interaction technique. For this reason, when designing a multitouch-enabled application, an easy and intuitive interaction scheme is a must. Users want to open the application and start using it with little or no training, also in the case of 3D applications.

Starting from the well known *virtual trackball* [18] approach, our design for the *MeshLab for iOS* app required to replace the well-known *mouse-based interface* with a more modern and intuitive *touch-based* interaction. Focusing on the single object inspection task allows us to exploit at best the directness supported by the touch-screen interaction. A set of interaction gestures was designed and implemented (see Figure 4): a *one-finger-drag* gesture allows to orbit around the object, thus controlling the three DOF of rotation; a *two-finger-drag* gesture is adopted to drive X- and Y-axis translations; a *two-fingers shrink/pull-apart* gestures perform uniform scaling; a *two-finger rotate* gesture achieves local Z-axis rotation; and, finally, a *single-finger double-tap* performs a change-of-focus operation, bringing the tapped point of the 3Dnsurface in the center of the screen and zooming on it. These gestures come across as 'natural' because each finger interacting with the touchscreen correlates directly with the underlying 3D model visualized on the display or, in the case of the orbit operation, with a spherical proxy object that acts as a handle for the rotation of the model.

The touch-based interfaces are becoming predominant also in the web-browsing environment; for this reason, also for the web-based visualization schemes we had to consider the implication of this change. While most of the advantages of the multi-touch interface are filtered by the browser, it is nevertheless true that an interface designed for a *mouse plus keyboard* interaction will perform poorly on a touch-only device. For example, when designing the interface of a WebGL/SpiderGL component, it is necessary to consider that the user might not have a keyboard available (and thus we should provide an alternative for modifier keys), that the visual elements (like buttons) used in the interaction should have at least the size of a finger and a decent spacing, and that some interaction methods (like the double click/tap) are easier than other (the right click).

In terms of usability, the results of some preliminary informal tests of *MeshLab for iOS* performed with CH users (scholars, students or restorers) produced an excellent evaluation. We experimented that users become able to manipulate a virtual object much faster with the touch-based approach than with the usual mouse-based interface provided by the desktop version of MeshLab.

The second research line mentioned above was aimed at the design of specific constrained interactions rules, to be used in all those cases where we think the user should not be allowed to perform generic manipulations. For example, if our artwork is a statue, it could be useful to constrain the manipulation by forcing the virtual statue to keep its vertical orientation (forbidding to rotate the head below the body). This has been implemented, for example, in the browser designed to inspect the Ruthwell Cross (see Figure 5 and [22]), where the user is forced to keep the cross in its vertical disposition. In this case, visual inspection is structured in a cylindrical fashion: right and left mouse drags produce a rotation around the object, while the up and down drags shift the cross vertically along its axis. The choice of a constrained navigation, while somehow limiting the possible viewpoints, greatly simplifies the visualization of an object by providing an interaction that is tailored to its shape. Therefore, we can envision that a generic browser could be defined by supporting different constrained interaction rules, each one best fitting some specific type of object: nearly planar for such artifacts as bas-reliefs; turntable or simplified trackballs for standard 3D objects that we might be interested in inspecting from any side;

mostly linearly-constrained for objects that have a decoration that follows a specific path (e.g. the Trajan column, where one could be interested in following a spiral navigation path that follows the carved decoration); etc. Selecting the proper interaction rule could be a task for the multimedia designer of the specific multimedia presentation, or it could be left accessible to users as an available option.

4   Integration of Different Media – The 3D Model as the Spatial Index to Knowledge

In CH applications, 3D models are major assets to:

- Document an artwork
- Assess the conservation status
- Present the status before and after a restoration
- Disseminate to the large public

Any project, being it devoted to the study of an artwork or to its restoration, produces an incredible corpus of data. This includes historical documents, texts, natural images, and the results of scientific investigations (that are encoded, again, with texts, images or graphs). This complex pool of **data associated to / interlinked with** the 3D model is usually returned and archived as a set of disconnected multimedia documents, usually stored in different places. Those data layers represent the knowledge over a given artwork: retrieving them and establishing all the required connections between those data is a complex, time consuming and valuable work that is usually lost at the end of a project (since the final result is still usually a written report or a book). Ideally, those data should be preserved, enriched by the associated metadata, and access should be granted to all scholars/students/amateurs. Any technological tool that will support the open access to and the easy delivery of those knowledge layers will make a major contribution to a more modern management policy of CH knowledge.

In this framework, the *digital 3D model* can be used to build up **spatial indexes** and to work as the **supporting media** to present other types and sources of information. We have seen that we have new and sufficiently consolidated solutions for distributing and using 3D data on the web (Section 2). Visualization of high-quality 3D models is possible but the required features are not just limited to the interactive visualization / navigation; conversely, we need authoring tools able to enrich the 3D model with hotspots, selection of views and links to other multimedia assets (images, text, graphics, video, audio, etc.) [19]. For this purpose, we must go beyond basic visualization of 3D models and build applications that link the 3D model to the other media, supporting the construction of web presentations that allow an interactive, integrated and efficient access to an entire corpus of knowledge.

A first step in this direction could be to design web pages where the 3D model stores a number of links on its surface, each one pointing to a specific chunk of information that can be activated and visualized with a simple click [20, 21]. The Community Presenter tools (Sect. 2.3) already supports the construction of multimedia applications where the 3D model could play the role of a spatial index to other type of information elements, by adding hot spots and hypermedia links to other information tokens (text, images, videos, etc.).

A more sophisticated result could be obtained by designing a system able to interconnect different media and to provide a complex network of cross-links and relations. A first attempt on this path has been done recently with the design of a system able to provide a strict correlation between *text* and *3D models* [22]. Many CH artworks are very complex and require long and structured textual descriptions to tell their story, to explain the artistic value and the iconographic content. We usually have to present a story that is narrated by means of the sculpted decorations (in the case of statues, bas-reliefs or even buildings). We cannot just focus on the text or on the visual channel: we should have both media available at the same time, with a tight synchronization in the navigation over each media. Therefore, our goal was to design a modular, extensible framework for the presentation and navigation of interconnected 3D models and textual information, where the user can explore the content in a completely free fashion, or could refer to a set of reference points that link each portion of the textual description to the corresponding ideal view over the 3D model (and vice versa). Some images of the prototype of this system are presented in Figure 5.

The Ruthwell Cross (http://en.wikipedia.org/wiki/Ruthwell_Cross) is the artwork selected as test bed for the design and assessment of our browser. The Ruthwell Cross is an Anglo-Saxon stone cross that presents a number of issues and is thus ideal as a test bed since:

1. It is a large artwork (5.5 meters high) with a lot of carved details on its surface that depict Christ and several other figures;
2. The stone surface is carved, irregular and highly degraded in several regions;
3. The carved figures and decorations have an important symbolic and religious meaning that requires textual descriptions to explain that content to non-experts;
4. Runic inscriptions are carved on the side of several of the carved figures, and require transcriptions and explanations.

Points 1 and 2 are issues that require the adoption of a browser able to present all the richness of a high-resolution model (the full resolution model of the Ruthwell Cross produced with 3D scanning is described by 122 M triangles). Points 3 and 4 suggest the combined use of visual and text media in the presentation of the artwork.

The basic idea is to use different representations of an artwork (possibly including different media), each one annotated, in the sense that each specific point of of the surface of the artwork is associated to a unique ID. If we have several *"models"* representing the artwork (for example a 3D model, an image, a text), each ID can be found in some or all those representations, thus providing a "connection point" which can be used by the user to move seamlessly from one media to another one. Our browsing system therefore should provide a series of viewers, which are HTML/JavaScript objects, each one able to:

• Visualize a specific kind of media/dataset;
• Show the available connection points (and let the user select each of them);
• Move the visualization focus to one specific connection point, according to the request of any other viewer (to synchronize the visualization of the different media).

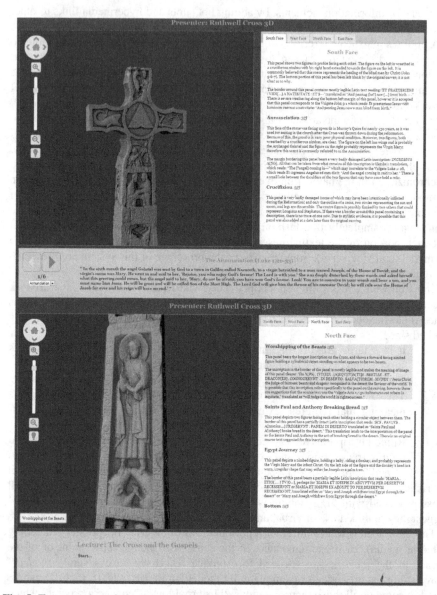

Fig. 5. Two snapshots from our web-based presentation systems, developed on top of Nexus and SpiderGL, that allows to present in an integrated manner a complex artwork, the Ruthwell Cross, by means of interrelated textual descriptions and 3D visualization

The underlying structure needed to synchronize the visualization is basically a dictionary containing the IDs and a map of the annotated datasets, that will act as a synchronization agent. The final user will be able to browse each representation in its specific viewer and, when selecting one of the connection points, synchronize all the other viewers in the page, to continue the exploration over another media or just to have in foreground the point of interest.

When designing a visualization web page, the author can assemble multiple viewers in the page, to cope with the needs of the project. The various datasets are fed into the system using XML configuration files; with such a separation between the visualization code and the data, it is possible to build different web-based visualization schemes without having to modify JavaScript code, but just authoring the XML content, a task suitable also for non programmers.

While our prototype [22] is at the moment limited to textual and 3D representations, it is based on a general concept of free and synchronized exploration of an artwork across all its representations and it can be further extended to other media (a set of photos, videos, technical drawings and surveys).

This system has been developed with the idea of using it as an educational tool: a sort of interactive multimedia textbook, usable in a class to present a specific artifact or, later on, to support the student/scholar when studying the object. To strengthen this idea, we added to the system another component whose purpose is to present a specific, annotated, exploration path of the available datasets that uses the available connection points (see the grey bar on the bottom of the window in Figure 5). We believe that this component may be extremely useful for a teacher when preparing and presenting a lesson or for a student when preparing and presenting an essay.

5   Conclusions

The delivery of informative rich and high resolution three-dimensional content on the web and on mobile devices has been an open issue for a long time, due to the lack of standards, practices and because of hardware limitations. The improvements and novelties that appeared in the last few years have finally opened new perspectives for a full integration of 3D contents in the everyday life of users and in some important professional contexts, like Cultural Heritage.

We have presented a number of new technologies, encompassing efficient multiresolution representation and rendering solutions, for both local and web-based visual presentation, together with technologies for an improved interaction with those multimedia models, covering also the domain of touch-based platforms. Finally, we have briefly touched the integration issue, demonstrating how the multimedia technologies could be extended to support the capability of interlinking and integrating different media.

All those technologies give us impressing and unprecedented capabilities for documenting CH artworks and for telling their story. Their potential impact on the way we perceive and we are educated on artistic themes is impressive. Those technologies could bring a revolution in the way people document, communicate or teach arts. Even if technologies are now starting to be mature, there have been limited efforts so far with respect to large scale deployment and assessment efforts. Two current EU projects (the NoE "V-MUST" - http://www.v-must.net/ - and the infrastructure project "ARIADNE" - http://www.ariadne-infrastructure.eu/) will give us an ideal framework for producing cutting edge experiments for a larger scale dissemination and assessments of these integrated technologies.

Moreover, other potential directions of work, exploiting new technologies like natural interfaces and immersive 3D visualization, could provide additional breakthroughs concerning user immersion and usability.

Acknowledgments. This work has been partially partially founded by the European Projects Ariadne (FP7–INFRA–2012–1–313193) and NoE V-MUST.Net (FP7 *Grant Agreement no. 270404*).

References

1. Callieri, M., Cignoni, P., Corsini, M., Scopigno, R.: Masked photo blending: mapping dense photographic dataset on high-resolution sampled 3D models. Computers and Graphics 32(4), 464–473 (1981)
2. Dellepiane, M., Marroquim, R., Callieri, M., Cignoni, P., Scopigno, R.: Flow-Based Local Optimization for Image-to-Geometry Projection. IEEE Transactions onVisualization and Computer Graphics 18(3), 463–474 (2012)
3. Lensch, H.P.A., Kautz, J., Goesele, M., Heidrich, W., Seidel, H.-P.: Image-based reconstruction of spatial appearance and geometric detail. ACM Transaction on Graphics 22, 234–257 (2003)
4. Scopigno, R., Callieri, M., Cignoni, P., Corsini, M., Dellepiane, M., Ponchio, F., Ranzuglia, G.: 3D models for Cultural Heritage: beyond plain visualization. IEEE Computer 44(7), 48–55 (2011)
5. Corsini, M., Dellepiane, M., Dercks, U., Ponchio, F., Keultjes, D., Marinello, A., Sigismondi, R., Scopigno, R., Wolf, G.: CENOBIUM - Putting Together the Romanesque Cloister Capitals of the mediterranean region. B.A.R. - British Archaeological Reports International Series, vol. 2118, pp. 189–194. Archaeopress (2010)
6. Kim, M.H., Rushmeier, H.E., French, J., Passeri, I.: Developing Open-Source Software for Art Conservators. In: VAST 2012 Proc., Eurographics, pp. 97–104 (2012)
7. Borgeat, L., Godin, G., Blais, F., Massicotte, P., Lahanier, C.: GoLD: interactive display of huge colored and textured models. ACM Trans. Graph. 24(3), 869–877 (2005)
8. Wimmer, M., Scheiblauer, C.: Instant points: fast rendering of unprocessed point clouds. In: Proceedings of the 3rd Eurographics / IEEE VGTC Conference on Point-Based Graphics, SPBG 2006 (2006)
9. Cignoni, P., Ganovelli, F., Gobbetti, E., Marton, F., Ponchio, F., Scopigno, R.: Adaptive tetrapuzzles: Efficient out-of-core construction and visualization of gigantic multiresolution polygonal models. ACM Trans. on Graphics (SIGGRAPH 2004) 23(3), 796–803 (2004)
10. Cignoni, P., Ganovelli, F., Gobbetti, E., Marton, F., Ponchio, F., Scopigno, R.: Batched multi triangulation. In: IEEE Visualization 2005, pp. 27–35 (2005)
11. Khronos Group. WebGL - OpenGL ES 2.0 for the Web (2009)
12. Behr, J., Eschler, P., Jung, Y., Zollner, M.: X3DOM: a DOM-based HTML5/X3D integration model. In: Proceedings of the 14th International Conference on 3D Web Technology (Web3D 2009), pp. 127–135 (2009)

13. Di Benedetto, M., Ponchio, F., Ganovelli, F., Scopigno, R.: SpiderGL: A JavaScript 3D Graphics Library for Next-Generation WWW. In: 15th Conference on 3D Web Technology, Web3D Consortium, ACM Web3D 2010, pp. 165–174 (2010)

14. Palma, G., Siotto, E., Proesmans, M., Baldassari, M., Baracchini, C., Batino, S., Scopigno, R.: Telling The Story of Ancient Coins By Means Of Interactive RTI Images Visualization. In: CAA 2012 Proceedings of the 40th Conference in Computer Applications and Quantitative Methods in Archaeology, Southampton, United Kingdom, March 26-30 (2012)

15. Christie, M., Olivier, P., Normand, J.-M.: Camera control in computer graphics. Computer Graphics Forum 27(8), 2197–2218 (2008)

16. Khan, A., Mordatch, I., Fitzmaurice, G., Matejka, J., Kurtenbach, G.: ViewCube: a 3D orientation indicator and controller. In: Proceedings of the 2008 Symposium on Interactive 3D Graphics and Games (I3D 2008), pp. 17–25. ACM, New York (2008)

17. Fitzmaurice, G., Matejka, J., Mordatch, I., Khan, A., Kurtenbach, G.: Safe 3D navigation. In: Proceedings of the 2008 Symposium on Interactive 3D Graphics and Games (I3D 2008), pp. 7–15. ACM, New York (2008)

18. Chen, M., Mountford, S.J., Sellen, A.: A study in interactive 3D rotation using 2D control devices. In: Proceedings of the 15th Annual Conference on Computer Graphics and Interactive Techniques, SIGGRAPH 1988, pp. 121–129. ACM, New York (1988)

19. Faraday, P., Sutcliffe, A.: Designing effective multimedia presentations. In: Proceedings of the ACM SIGCHI Conference on Human Factors in Computing Systems (CHI 1997), pp. 272–278. ACM, New York (1997)

20. Jankowski, J., Samp, K., Irzynska, I., Jozwowicz, M., Decker, S.: Integrating Text with Video and 3D Graphics: The Effects of Text Drawing Styles on Text Readability. In: Proceedings of the SIGCHI Conference on Human Factors in Computing Systems (CHI 2010), pp. 1321–1330. ACM, New York (2010)

21. Polys, N.F., Bowman, D.A., North, C.: The role of Depth and Gestalt cues in information-rich virtual environments. Int. J. Hum.-Comput. Stud. 69(1-2), 30–51 (2011)

22. Callieri, M., Leoni, C., Dellepiane, M., Scopigno, R.: Artworks narrating a story: a modular framework for the integrated presentation of three-dimensional and textual contents. In: Proceedings of the ACM 18th International Conference on 3D Web Technology, Web3D 2013 (2013) (in press)

23. Koller, D., Frischer, B., Humphreys, G.: Research challenges for digital archives of 3D cultural heritage models. ACM J. Computing and Cult. Herit. 2(3), Article 7 (January 2010)

24. Patel, M., White, M., Mourkoussis, N., Walczak, K., Wojciechowski, R., Chmielewski, J.: Metadata requirements for digital museum environments. International Journal on Digital Libraries 5(3), 179–192 (2005)

Geometry vs Semantics: Open Issues on 3D Reconstruction of Architectural Elements

Livio De Luca[1] and David Lo Buglio[1,2]

[1] UMR 3495 CNRS / MCC MAP Gamsau - Marseille, France
{livio.deluca,david.lobuglio}@map.archi.fr
[2] Laboratoire AlICe - Faculté d'Architecture La Cambre Horta,
Université Libre de Bruxelles (ULB) – Brussel, Belgium
david.lo.buglio@ulb.ac.be

Abstract. Three-dimensional representation is becoming an effective support for the documentation of the state of conservation of heritage artefacts, for the study of its transformations and for cultural diffusion. 3D digitization technologies now offer effective means to observe and analyze historic buildings with more accuracy, completeness and timeliness. Nevertheless, this produces a real problem of information overload. The growing mass of un-interpreted data make emerge a need for innovative methodologies assisting data processing, sorting and analysis by researchers who want to use it for advancing the knowledge of cultural heritage. Exploring the informational value of these new representation systems allows introducing new approaches to the analysis of artefacts so distant in space but so close in features (typologies, styles, compositional rules, etc.). This chapter presents some research avenues for defining a geometric/semantic description model of architectural elements in order to integrate the informative value of 3D digitization in intelligible representations.

Keywords: Architecture, heritage, representation, 3D digitization, epistemology, knowledge, geometry, semantics.

1 Introduction

During the past three decades, the fields concerning heritage documentation took advantage of digital and survey techniques development. One can consider that this development has been done in favour of acquisition and processing work (in order to reconstruct and document complex architectural objects). The realization of 3D models of heritage buildings in their current state, as the hypothetical reconstruction of past states, requires a powerful methodology able to not only capture and digitally reconstruct fine geometric details and appearances of such objects, but also to interpret their morphology in order to compose intelligible representations. Nowadays, 3D data is a critical component to permanently record the shape of impor- tant objects and sites so that, at least in digital form, they might be handed down to future generations. Reality-based 3D modeling today has become an effective solution for providing dense and accurate 3D representations which are the basis for further uses such as

M. Ioannides and E. Quak (Eds.): 3D Research Challenges, LNCS 8355, pp. 36–49, 2014.
© Springer-Verlag Berlin Heidelberg 2014

documentation material production, restoration and conservation policies, physical replicas, digital inventories, etc. Various tools and emerging technologies [1], [2] have been integrated into approaches for the 3D reconstruction of buildings in order to reproduce the morphological complexity of heritage buildings and to support different analysis requirements [3].

If the (constantly growing) mass of data has effectively enabled to approach the reconstruction of complex geometries, this overgrowth (of data) does not seem to increase the level of intelligibility of the representations produced.

The scientific analysis of documentary resources has benefited from informatics solutions regarding the organization and management of data. Many solutions have been developed in order to improve the management of digital contents using a formal structure for describing implicit and explicit concepts and relations used in cultural heritage documentation [4].

If much of the work has focused on the semantic characterization of generic 3D shapes [5], very little seems to deal with integrating heterogeneous data in a display device referring to the building morphology [6]. Solutions that could be applied to this problem are certainly GIS (geographical information system) and BIM (building information modeling) systems. However, in order to conceive an information system for the study of heritage buildings that is able to really exploit the potential of reality-based 3D representations, a more profound analysis of data structuring problems must be done.

In order to anticipate a foreseen methodological deficit, it is necessary to provide some reflections for the creation of representation systems that are able to enrich the informational value of the documents produced.

Behind the technical advances of 3D representation, many difficulties are arising with the creation, the sharing and the dissemination of digital models (models whose data continues to grow). This leaves open a field of epistemological questions on the practices of the architectural representation.

But more specifically, these questions must help to position the research beyond the simple purpose of development of tools and techniques, so it provides to the field of heritage documentation methodological reflections on the scientific issues surrounding the representation of artefacts.

The study of means must also pay attention to the specific cognitive issues belonging to the architectural representation in order to take into account the link between perception and the semiotic foundations of communication. This concern assumes that the representation of an architectural object cannot escape from our vision and for the knowledge we mobilize for its understanding.

We attempt here to provide reflection avenues for innovative development of representation systems (and information technologies) that can constitute new tools for investigation and scientific visualization, assuming the dimensions of "complexity" and "intelligibility" within the same graphical space.

Three-dimensional representation of the built environment is becoming an effective support for documenting architectural artefacts, study of built deteriorations, cultural diffusion and promotion of heritage. In this context, new technologies involved in 3D digitization give new means for observing built environment with more accuracy, more completeness and less time. However, the application of these new technologies produces a problem of "data" overload. The growing mass of points clouds, 3D models and un-interpreted data require innovative methodologies for knowledge processing, sorting and finally analysis.

After a brief assessment of the results obtained within the context of a critical study of the relationship between the 3D digitization of the built heritage and the informational contribution of digital models, we presented in a paper, some avenues of research in the fields of heritage representation [7]. More generally these tracks questioned the ability of representations to be transformed into tools of analysis, scientific evaluation and transmission of knowledge [8]. This transmission through the figure must be able to associate the specific knowledge available on the artefact with generic knowledge drawn from the theory of architecture [9].

2 Analysis of the Informational Value of Architectural Digital Representations

In order to meet the supposed "lack of" intelligibility deficit, we suggested a first approach to objectify the informational content of 3D digitization of architectural artefacts [7]. The first results of this critical analysis have enabled a better understanding of how certain modeling methods or digitization techniques contribute to improve the level of architectural knowledge transmitted by the representations produced. As it is difficult to imagine that the single use of technology can replace the cognitive contribution of a human operator, the study also suggested to evaluate the contribution of the operator in the semantic enrichment of the digital model.

The lasergrammetry and photogrammetry, as techniques for recording dimensional and colorimetric aspects of a building, are now used to reconstruct the visual appearance of complex architectural morphologies. With these advances, we might think that the representation of territory at a 1:1 scale suggested by Borges is not so far [10] and the technologies used in the survey campaigns seems to be the primary source of the enrichment of the architectural representation. However, these tools respond first to the requirements of accuracy and completeness and are far from the cognitive issues of the architectural representation [11]. These issues (surrounding the architectural representation) are based on a paradigm that exists since the Italian Renaissance and that considers the representation (in a survey process) as a space which overlays, via the figure, the specific and generic knowledge about the artefact.

To conduct this review on methodological aspects, the observations focused on a series of digitization works. The objective was to evaluate the set of information that describes the architectural object in order to measure the information gain provided by the document, regarding the employed requirements and means. The observation was conducted from automated reconstruction processes up to manual restitution works.

The mobilized criteria for the analysis were defined on the basis of an empirical observation of digitization works as well as on the concept of "informational modeling" developed by Blaise and Dudek [12]. Starting from this concept, they set forth certain methodological approaches to increase the intelligibility of the informational content of the 3D model. Beyond the facilities offered by this guide of "good practices" and by the logic of symmetry, these rules offer a legitimate theoretical basis to locate some informational properties of a representation.

Without going into detail, these observations have demonstrated a wider cognitive commitment of the operator as he approaches a manual restitution process. This relatively clear causality effect also indicates the existence of a double epistemological problem.

- *The distancing of the operator in an automated reconstruction process (photogrammetric or lasergrammetric reconstruction by polygonal meshing) leads to a gain of objectivity of the representation produced. In contrast, the use of technologies enabling high levels of precision does not seem to be a pledge of a substantial cognitive contribution.*
- *In parallel, the analytical mechanisms of reading and interpreting present in a "manual" restitution process induce a form of subjectivity. It presents also a great interest to the cognitive enrichment of the model. However, the digitization observed showed us that a representation that does not express the relative level of knowledge may hardly be used as a tool for scientific evaluation* [7].

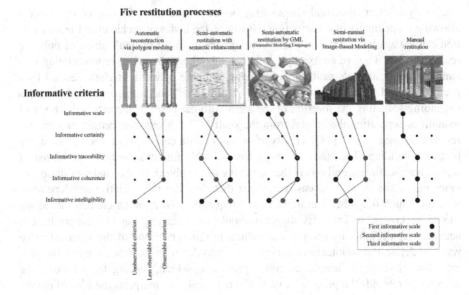

Fig. 1. Analysis of the information content of five restitution processes

1. Automatics reconstruction via polygon meshing [13]. Column of the Abbey of Saint-Guilhem-le-désert. Visual levels (geometry, textures, occlusion + textures).

2. Semi-automatic restitution with semantic enhancement [14]. Architectural semantisation of the point cloud of the Arc de Triomphe. See also Nubes project.

3. Semi-automatic restitution by GML [15]. Shape variation of a Gothic Window Tracery created in GML.

4. Semi-manual restitution via Image-Based Modeling. Image-based modeling of the current state of the refectory of Villers-la-Ville Abbey (Belgium). Digitization done by Laboratoire AlICe, Faculté d'Architecture La Cambre Horta, Université Libre de Bruxelles (ULB).

5. Manual restitution of the temple of Mars Ultor [16].

3   Between Complexity and Intelligibility

3.1   Modeling Semantically-Enriched 3D Architectural Shapes

The analysis of architectural shapes may be led by the identification of the process allowing its geometrical construction. However, the codes of architectural representation can always help in this stage, which remains the most difficult phase of building reconstruction. To give an example, one can take the geometrical representation of a simple column: this element, far from being a simple cylinder, is characterized by a pace (truncated, bent bottom, bent third, or reinflated) and transitions as the cimbia (moulding softening the meeting of the shaft with the base) or the astragale (body of mouldings separating the capital from the shaft [17]). Moreover, certain proportions regulate its dimensions [18]. This type of observation can be made for almost every part of a building. The study of shape has a double finality: the first one is that of representation, the second one is the surveying of the object. If one analyzes these two moments of the study, one easily realizes that they are in a strictly interdependent relation, which is neither hierarchical, nor sequential. To draw an element, its shape should be known, to know its shape, it should be measured, but to measure it, it is necessary to decipher its geometrical nature. In this sense, one of the most effective ways to define the architectural survey is to consider it as the rebuilding of the project. The surveying is indeed a reverse process in which, starting from an existing object, one rebuilds the process of its realization, and one interprets the idea of design which comes before its realization [19].

Within the logical continuity with the history of the architectural representation, our general purpose consists of considering the digital surveying of an historic building as a cognitive act: the moment in which one can analyse relevant relations between shape, geometry and architectural sense. Our works start from the idea that even if today one can use new (and sophisticated) tools, specific requirements coming from the architectural documentation and conservation fields remain and need the development of "intelligible" representations. In this sense, the alignment of emerging techniques to conventional codes of architectural representation is a main issue.

The application of geometry to the description and analysis of the architectural shape necessitates the reduction of multiplicity into intelligibility. Examples of this approach may be found in various fields and applied to the geometrical understanding of shapes or varied phenomena [20]. In the same way, starting from a geometrical analysis of the various parts of a building, and by having as an objective its geometrical and semantic description, we proposed a method for the geometrical reconstruction starting from profiles [21]. This method is founded on the analysis of invariant and morphological specificities one can extract from a semantic segmentation of the building morphology. Throughout the history of architecture, the morphological complexity of shapes was always influenced by the methods of geometrical control that made their conception possible; examples of these methods are the descriptive geometry [22] or stereotomy [23], [24]. Based on a study of the principles subjacent to these control methods of architectural shape, one can then identify, on one side, relevant information to be extracted from survey (profiles in a point cloud for example) and, on the other side, the process of construction better adapted to ensure the geometrical restitution of elements.

Starting from this first issue, we worked on the definition of a generic formalism for the semantic representation of classical elements [25]. The approach we defined in order to describe architectural elements takes into account three distinct dimensions:

- The interpretation of knowledge relating to shapes
- The definition of methods allowing their geometrical modeling
- The identification of the relations between the sub-parts of shapes

We organize the formalization of the element according to relations between two parallel levels of description: geometrical and semantic. The first makes it possible to rebuild shapes in three dimensions; the second makes it possible to organize parts according to the vocabulary of the architect. Geometrical description is based on the relations among three types of generic nodes (conceptual elements of the formalism) describing the construction of the element from the definition of its geometrical atoms (lowest-level geometrical entities) to the complete generation of its surfaces.

- Atoms: a node characterized by a structure of information concerning the geometrical construction, the spatial transformation and the constraints of an atomic entity.
- Profiles: a level, which allows the grouping of the mouldings according to the construction plans.
- Surfaces: a level which uses specific nodes for the generation of surfaces starting from profiles

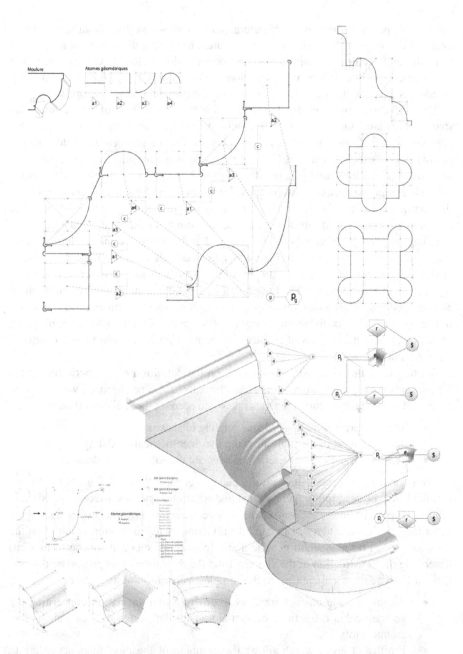

Fig. 2. Atoms, profiles and surfaces of the generic formalism for the geometric description of classical elements

These atoms are the only entities of the formalization for which we provide geometrical information (control points of a line or of a curve): indeed, the generation of the whole element surface is based exclusively on constraint relations, grouping operations and modeling functions. Figure 2 shows the geometrical construction of a doric capital described in Palladio's treaty [8] and obtained by a simple combination of geometrical atoms gathered in two generating profiles and extruded along two directing paths. For the formalization of the element we connect atoms according to the sequence of mouldings. Once mouldings are suitably proportioned (introducing dimensional values), we gather them in two generating profile nodes according to the respective modeling procedures. The semantic description level is defined by a structure of concepts organized around the geometrical description. Nodes of the semantic description, on one side, are connected to architectural terms, and on the other, gather the geometrical description elements in a hierarchical structure: atoms/mouldings/parts of the profile. We use formalized primitives in order to constitute a library of architectural elements by the simple declaration of a sequence of mouldings (see Fig. 3)

Fig. 3. Bases and balusters modelled by declaration of a sequence of geometrical atoms

3.2   Reasoning from Semantics to Geometry and Vice-Versa

The potential of the image-based 3D reconstruction approaches with respect to range-based / LiDAR methods is getting more and more evident, thanks to the latest developments in dense image matching [26], [27], [28], [29], [30] and the availability of web-based and open-source processing tools (e.g. Photosynth, 123DCatch, Apero, MicMac, etc.). These developments based on photogrammetry and computer vision methods have shown very promising results and renewed attention for image-based 3D modeling as an inexpensive, robust and practical alternative to 3D scanning.

The introduction of new protocols for acquisition and processing of spatial data [31] has given rise to new research perspectives. The opportunity to combine records, geometric analysis and characterisations about several artefacts could also be used for developing new approaches for shape classification and interpretation. The availability of flexible solutions for collecting morphological data on masses of artefacts allow considering the shape analysis as a fundamental moment for reasoning about the relationships between geometry and semantics and in a bidirectional analysis approach.

In the first case (from semantics to geometry), the idea is to explore ways to insert architectural semantics within the surveying procedures (by associating them with dimensional information). This would allow an immediate reading of dimensional parameters corresponding to architectural concepts that characterize the artefact (see fig. 4).

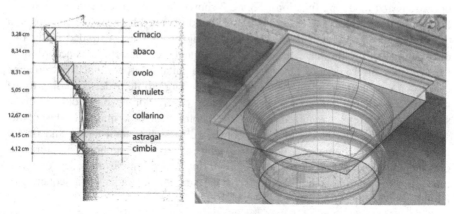

Fig. 4. Primitive adjusted on the point cloud. On the left, vertical profile with dimensional information; on the right, primitive projected on a photography oriented on the point cloud.

This kind of approach can provide great advantages in the 3D reconstruction process. A correct (and knowledge-based) interpretation of data prevents the production of unrealistic architectural shapes and would provide models linked to specific vocabularies and grammars. Indeed, we believe that the modeling of architectural elements must refer to the formal description of characters defined by the codes of architectural representation (in relation to historical periods and stylistic trends). In this context, significant efforts on formalizing typical architectural elements can be conducted, including the study and re-interpretation (in the context of the digital modelling domain) of architectural treatises (description of typical shapes, compositional rules, constraints of positioning and orientation, principles of scaling, etc..).

In the second case (from geometry to semantics) it's necessary to investigate solutions for the shape segmentation but also the issues related to semantic annotation. Indeed, for some years now the communities involved in the heritage documentation seem gradually take over the problems related to intelligibility deficit. There are now numerous studies concerned with the exploitation of non-interpreted data. Indeed, the geometric description and the analysis of architectural shapes require a reduction of multiplicity to intelligibility.

We recently started working on a shape analysis method combining a bottom-up approach, in which the meaning of the elements comes from the combination of a low-level, and a top-down morphological analysis, which takes advantage of pre-structured knowledge (see Fig. 5).

This kind of approach is therefore based on the identification of generic models that can integrate multiple instances (e.g. objects belonging to the same stylistic trend) by bringing out common morphological features by means of the identification of semantic /geometric classes.

The digital segmentation of architectural digitization could follow a top-down approach, which takes advantage of pre-structured knowledge of the domain or bottom-up approach, in which the meaning of the elements comes from a "free" morphological analysis. Concerning the top-down approach, it is necessary to study the techniques of semi-automatic segmentation in order to identify meaningful parts

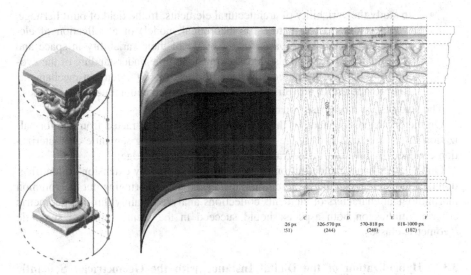

Fig. 5. Generation of a depth map from the polygonal mesh and analysis of geometric discontinuities and profiles directly on the map

(a base, a shaft and a capital of a column) corresponding to well-defined concepts (in terms of architectural vocabulary). The transfer of segmentation and semantic annotation to unique items, even to the entire model, is studied a second time. The study on segmentation and semantic annotation should complement an analysis of the geometric similarity used to compare elements or architectural objects between them. This would create a library of architectural forms and morphological criteria organized around pre-structured knowledge.

As it is explained above, it seems also necessary to complete this first step with a bottom-up approach that would take advantage of the multiplicity of acquired data. In this case, the meaning of the elements would come from a "free" morphological estimation and not from a shape thesaurus. The "free" estimation corresponds to the opportunity to study without bias on the results, the point aggregate, the curvatures of surfaces and volumes of the architectural elements.

The use of statistical analysis would permit to find correspondences between different geometric entities. Morphological comparisons that can be done on a set of shapes offer opportunities to study similarities in a collection of architectural elements (Fig. 6). Indeed, by establishing common geometric observation criteria and multiplying comparisons between elements, it is possible to identify morphological signatures that can contribute, in a second step, at the semantic characterization of a collection. This approach is therefore based on the self-expansion of a large amount of data. The medium-term challenges of this approach are:

- to establish new shape classification criteria. The comparison of architectural objects on the basis of geometric similarities aims to create libraries of architectural shapes organized around pre-structured knowledge.
- to question architectural treaties with the classification work (through the geometrical analysis of the typical shapes, the composition rules, the principles of scale, the positioning constraints, the orientation, etc...).

- to study the variability of architectural elements. In the field of built heritage, the morphological signature (or theoretical model) of a collection of elements can serve as the basis for the study of their variability in space and time. In addition, it can also have an impact on the understanding of the evolution of a style. In the continuation, the use of self-extension mechanisms can provide useful answers to observe unclassified and uninterpreted shapes.

The study is therefore based on a dual approach.

On the one hand, the study of the typical characteristics extracted from the formalization of architectural knowledge associated with an existing semantic characterization conduct "by intention" (integration of pre-defined knowledge);

On the other hand, the definition of an analysis strategy "by extension" (identification of a model that can integrate multiple instances) able of bringing out the common morphological characters of elements collections analyzed mainly through geometric criteria. Studies on both aspects should succeed in the identification of semantic /geometric classes.

3.3 Hybridization of the Digital Instance with the Geometrical/ Semantic Model in a 3D Representation

As it is written in the introduction, digitization generally responds to one of these two concepts: multiplicity or intelligibility. If the multiplicity refers to un-interpreted and visible digital instance of the architectural object, the notion of intelligibility cross-reference to the theoretical model of the same object. In other words, it expresses

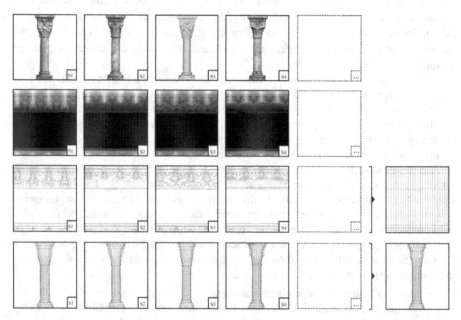

Fig. 6. A comparative analysis of four columns : from left to right, the polygonal mesh, the produced depth map, the extracted discontinuities, the created simplified geometric reconstruction and the average values

its ability to evoke a universe of knowledge that can inform us about the semantic construction of an architectural element. The shift from multiplicity to intelligibility presupposes the presence of a human operator whose aim is to filter, reduce and interpret all data collected in order to retain only those which will replenish the theoretical model. This is essential to produce a set of relevant information in relation to the analytical objectives pursued.

But beyond the analytical issues, it is necessary to think about the distance between the instance and its theoretical model, and how these two concepts can be articulated in a unique representation system.

It would be interesting to define a geometric/semantic model allowing a hybridization of the complexity (representing instances without interpretation) with semantic concepts (linked to the notion of intelligibility). The suggested procedure (see Fig. 7) thus follows these steps [32]:

- Interactive and semi-automatic 3D reconstruction based on several methods that depend directly on the morphological complexity:
- Basic adaptation of geometric primitives on an extension from the geometry (bottom) to architecture (up).
- Computing a disparity map between the original item (dense points cloud or polygons) and the simplified elements (primitive, lightweight mesh, etc.).
- Mapping of visual and geometric information (from the original elements) on the simplified elements by creating "enriched textures" (depending on the UV setting).

Fig. 7. Process of mapping visual information and geometry on geometric primitives through the creation of "enriched textures"

4   Conclusions

Based on a partial assessment of methodological deficiencies surrounding the techniques and methods of architectural heritage digitization, this chapter highlights various indicators to better assess the informational value of an architectural representation. But beyond this first aspect, this study has two objectives. First, it brings out the cognitive dimension present in the digitization work and second, it attempts to establish the relationship between the concepts of multiplicity of data and the intelligibility of the theoretical model.

The studies about the instance similarities or detailed digitization from simplified geometrical/semantic models constitute a relevant research avenue allowing to visualize the gap between a theoretical model and a digital instance. On the other hand, this approach opens up interesting prospects for a closer connection between the detailed documentation of an architectural object and its description in an analytic language (parametric). In other words, it helps to consider the description of an object in a language that separates the formal analysis from the visible form.

References

1. Boehler, W., Marbs, A.: 3D scanning instruments. In: Proceedings of the CIPA WG 6th Int. Workshop on Scanning for Cultural Heritage, Corfu, Greece (2002)
2. Debevec, P., Taylor, C., Malik, J.: Modeling and rendering architecture from photographs: a hybrid geometry and image-based approach. In: Proceedings of SIGGRAPH, New Orleans, LA, pp. 11–20 (1996)
3. El Hakim, S., Beraldin, A., Picard, M., Vettore, A.: Effective 3D modeling of heritage sites. In: Proceedings of the 4th Int. Conf. on 3D Digital Imaging and Modeling, Canada, pp. 302–309 (2003)
4. Doer, M.: The CIDOC CRM: an ontological approach to semantic interoperability of metadata. AI Magazine, Special Issue 24(3), 75–92 (2003)
5. Attene, M., Robbiano, F., Spagnuolo, M., Falcidieno, B.: Characterization of 3D shape parts for semantic annotation. Computer Aided Des. 41(10), 756–763 (2009)
6. Manferdini, A.M., Remondino, F., Baldissini, S., Gaiani, M., Benedetti, B.: 3D modeling and semantic classification of archaeological finds for management and visualization in 3D archaeological databases. In: Proceedings of the 14th Int. Conf. on Virtual Systems and MultiMedia (VSMM), Cyprus, pp. 221–228 (2008)
7. Lo Buglio, D., De Luca, L.: Critical review of 3D digitization methods and techniques applied to the field of architectural heritage: methodological and cognitive issues. In: The 12th International Symposium on Virtual Reality, Archaeology and Cultural Heritage, Vast 2011, pp. 5–12. Eurographics press, Prato (2011)
8. Palladio, A.: The Four Books of Architecture. Dover Publications, New York (1965) (1750)
9. Blaise, J.-Y., Dudek, I.: Modélisation informationnelle: concepts fondamentaux. Visualiser pour raisonner sur des connaissances architecturales. MIA Journal 1, 143–154 (2006)
10. Borges, J.L.: De la rigueur de la science. In: L'auteur et autres textes, pp. 221–221. Gallimard, Paris (1982)
11. Mediati, D.: L'occhio sul mondo per una semiotica del punto di vista. Rubbettino, Soveria Mannelli (2008)
12. Blaise, J.-Y., Dudek, I.: Modélisation Informationnelle, Imprimerie du CNRS – Provence (2006)
13. De Luca, L., Driscu, T., Labrosse, D., Peyrols, E., Berthelot, M.: Digital Anastylosis of the cloister of Saint-Guilhem-le-Desert. In: Research in Interactive Design. Proceedings of IDMME-Virtual Concept 2008, Beijing, vol. 3 (2008)

14. UMR 3495 CNRS/MCC MAP Gamsau: Nubes project,
    `http://www.map.archi.fr/nubes/introduction/projet.htm` (find June 26, 2011)
15. Havemann, S., Fellner, D.: Generative parametric design of Gothic window tracery. In: Shape Modeling International, pp. 350–353 (2004)
16. Université de Caen De Caen Basse-Normandie: Projet de restitution. Le Plan de Rome.Restituer la Rome Antique,
    `http://www.unicaen.fr/cireve/rome/pdr_restitution.php?fichier=objectifs` (find June 3, 2011)
17. Perouse de Montclos, J.M.: Architecture vocabulaire: principes d'analyse scientifique. Imprimerie Nationale, Paris (1972)
18. Forssman, E.: Palladio e le colonne. Bollettino del Centro Internazionale di Studi di Architettura Andrea Palladio. Vicenza, Italy (1978)
19. Migliari, R., Docci, L.: Geometria e architettura. Gangemi, Rome (2000)
20. Thompson, D.: On Growth and Form. Cambridge University Press, Cambridge (1942)
21. De Luca, L.: Relevé et multi-représentations du patrimoine architectural. Définition d'une approche hybride de reconstruction 3D d'édifices. PhD Thesis, Arts et Métiers Paris Tech (CER d'Aix-en-Provence), Paris (2006)
22. Monge, G.: Géométrie descriptive. Bibliothèque Nationale de France (BNF), Paris (1799)
23. Desargues, G.: Bruillon projet d'exemple d'une manière universelle du S.G.D. Touchant la pratique du trait à preuves pour la coupe des pierres en architecture. Bibliothèque Nationale de France (BNF), Paris (1640)
24. Vallée, L.: Spécimen de coupe de pierres, contenant les principes généraux du trait et leur application aux murs, aux plate-bande, aux berceaux, aux voûtes sphériques, aux voûtes de révolution, aux voûtes à base polygonale. Bibliothèque Nationale de France (BNF), Paris (1853)
25. De Luca, L., Veron, P., Florenzano, M.: A generic formalism for the semantic modeling and representation of architectural elements. The Visual Computer 23(3), 181–205 (2007)
26. Hirschmueller, H.: Stereo processing by semi-global matching and mutual information. IEEE Transactions on Pattern Analysis and Machine Intelligence 30(2), 328–341 (2008)
27. Remondino, F., El-Hakim, S., Gruen, A., Zhang, L.: Development and performance analysis of image matching for detailed surface reconstruction of heritage objects. IEEE Signal Processing Magazine 25(4), 55–65 (2008)
28. Hiep, V.H., Keriven, R., Labatut, P., Pons, J.P.: Towards high-resolution large-scale multiview stereo. In: Proceedings CVPR, Kyoto, Japan (2009)
29. Furukawa, Y., Ponce, J.: Accurate, dense and robust multiview stereopsis. IEEE Transactions on Pattern Analysis and Machine Intelligence 32(8), 1362–1376 (2010)
30. Jachiet, A.L., Labatut, P., Pons, J.P.: Robust piecewise-planar 3D reconstruction and completion from large-scale unstructured point data. In: Proceedings CVPR, San Francisco, USA (2010)
31. Pierrot-Deseilligny, M., De Luca, L., Remondino, F.: Automated Image-Based Procedures for Accurate Artifacts 3D Modeling and Orthoimage. In: XXIIIth International CIPA Symposium (2011)
32. Remondino, F., Lo Buglio, D., Nony, N., De Luca, L.: Detailed primitive-based 3d modeling of architectural elements. In: Proceedings of The XXII Congress of the International Society for Photogrammetry and Remote Sensing, Melbourne, Australia (2012)

3D Shape Analysis for Archaeology

Ayellet Tal

Technion
Haifa, Israel
ayellet@ee.technion.ac.il

Abstract. Archaeology is rapidly approaching an impasse in its ability to handle the overwhelming amount and complexity of the data generated by archaeological research. In this paper, we describe some results of our efforts in developing automatic shape analysis techniques for supporting several fundamental tasks in archaeology. These tasks include documentation, looking for corollaries, and restoration. We assume that the input to our algorithms is 3D scans of archaeological artifacts. Given these scans, we describe three techniques of documentation, for producing 3D visual descriptions of the scans, which are all non-photorealistic. We then proceed to explain our algorithm for partial similarity of 3D shapes, which can be used to query databases of shape, searching for corollaries. Finally, within restoration, we describe our results for digital completion of broken 3D shapes, for reconstruction of 3D shapes based on their line drawing illustrations, and for restoration of colors on 3D objects. We believe that when digital archaeological reports will spread around the globe and scanned 3D representations replace the 2D ones, our methods will not only accelerate, but also improve the results obtained by the current manual procedures.

1 Introduction

Shape analysis aims at developing efficient algorithms and technologies for "understanding" shapes. In this work we assume that a shape is a surface, represented as a "polygonal soup", which is the common representation in computer graphics in general, and the output of 3D scanners in particular.

The field of shape analysis tackles a whole spectrum of intriguing problems, including matching [1–3], segmentation [4–6], registration[7, 8], edge detection [9–11], saliency detection [12–14], completion [15–17], and more. The common denominator of all these tasks is that humans perform them easily and naturally, often by using semantics and their knowledge. When attempting to perform the tasks automatically, however, we do not assume any knowledge and therefore, the only information available to us is the geometry of the surface. Can geometry alone provide us with sufficient data to perform these tasks? For instance, when looking for similar shapes, is similarity in the eye of the beholder? Or, can similarity be defined mathematically, based solely on the geometric features of the shape?

M. Ioannides and E. Quak (Eds.): 3D Research Challenges, LNCS 8355, pp. 50–63, 2014.
© Springer-Verlag Berlin Heidelberg 2014

There are numerous applications of 3D shape analysis, both within the field of computer graphics and in other domains, such as medicine, biology, architecture, and cultural heritage. This is so, because in all these fields the emerging technology of 3D scanning is gaining popularity. Once the objects are represented and visualized on the computer, the reasonable next task is to analyze them as well. In this paper we focus on cultural heritage, and in particular on archaeology.

The field of archaeology is rapidly approaching an impasse in its ability to handle the overwhelming amount and complexity of the data generated by past and on-going archaeological research. A typical excavation produces thousands of artifacts, and large stratigraphical excavations–oftentimes millions. Worldwide, current methods of recording, analysis, archiving and restoration of data can no longer cope with the higher resolution required. Moreover, in most cases, researchers cannot access all the objects themselves, as they are locked away in museums and various store-rooms.

We propose to replace some components of the tasks of the archaeologist by digital procedures. In particular, we concentrate on three tasks: documentation, looking for corollaries, and restoration. For each, we describe our efforts in automating the activity. We view this work as part of a world-wide effort to overcome the impasse created by current manual procedures [18–21].

Specifically, in Section 2 we discuss 3D visual representations, which can replace the 2D ones, currently utilized for documentation. We propose several techniques which enhance the 3D data and make it attractive for visualization. Then, in Section 3 we discuss search by partial similarity. When the digital reports contain searchable databases of shape information, the process of searching for corollaries will be reduced to querying multiple on-line databases. Finally, in Section 4, we describe our restoration results, focusing on digital completion of broken 3D shapes, on reconstruction of 3D shapes based on their line drawing illustrations, and on restoration of colors on 3D objects.

Digital archaeological reports are slowly spreading around the globe [22–26]. When scanned 3D representations replace the 2D ones, accurate, automatic methods for performing shape analysis tasks are likely to replace the labor-intensive procedures currently employed.

2 Documentation

Traditionally, artifacts are documented and published by conventionalized line drawings or 2D photographs. The line drawings are produced manually, by artists—an extremely time and money consuming procedure, prone to inaccuracies and biases. Furthermore, usually only one, and only seldom more views of the objects are illustrated in publications. The result is that not all the morphological information is recorded.

Lately, 3D scanning gets increasing popularity. Indeed, 3D images are accurate, simple, and relatively quick to generate. And, they retain all the information regarding the objects. However, they still do not convey the pertinent morphological structure in a manner that enables rapid and effortless visual recognition, which is important when objects are viewed en masse.

Non-photorealistic rendering can overcome these drawbacks [27]. This is supported by psychological scholarship that demonstrates the visual advantage of line drawings for real-time recognition, especially when texture and color are not available [28].

Our goal is therefore to combine the comprehensiveness, accuracy and efficiency of 3D scans with the eye-friendliness and the information conveyed of non-photorealistic rendering. We propose three manners to achieve that: 3D curve illustration, black & white coloring, and relief extraction. Since in all these cases, the procedures are performed in 3D, manipulation enables the archaeologist to visualize the important features, as if the artifact is held in his hand.

Curve Detection: Our goal is to mathematically define a family of curves, which enhance the important features of a given 3D object. Based on this definition, an algorithm for constructing the curves on triangular meshes is designed. Since archaeological artifacts are extremely noisy, the algorithm should be robust to noise.

Given a surface, we define in [29, 30] a new class of view-independent curves, termed the *demarcating curve* , as follows. Given a surface in 3D, we can imagine it locally as a terrain with ridges and valleys [31]. Intuitively, demarcating curves run on the slopes between the ridges and the valleys. A common way to model such a slope locally, is to model it as a step edge. Ridges, valleys and demarcating curves are parallel on the step edge. The demarcating curve demarcates the concave part of the step edge from the convex part.

Formally, the demarcating curves are the loci of points for which there is a zero crossing of the curvature in the curvature gradient direction. This curvature gradient points in the direction of the fastest transition from concave to convex. Thus, $\mathbf{p}$ is a demarcating curve point if the following formula holds:

$$\kappa(\mathbf{g}_p) = \mathbf{g}_p{}^T \mathbf{II} \mathbf{g}_p = 0,$$

where $\mathbf{g}_p$, the curvature gradient, is defined as:

$$\mathbf{g}_p = \arg\max_{\mathbf{v}} \mathbf{C}_{ijk} \mathbf{v}^i \mathbf{v}^j \mathbf{v}^k, \quad \text{s.t } \|\mathbf{v}\| = 1.$$

Figure 1 demonstrates that our demarcating curves effectively manage to capture 3D shape information visually. They depict the 3D texture of an object, such as the facial features and the hair.

Coloring: In order to further highlight the features, it is possible to add surface enhancement to the demarcating curves. The key idea is to color the surface according to its normal curvature in the curvature gradient direction. This coloring increases the color contrast on the feature curves, thus enhancing them. In particular, Figure 1(c) demonstrates the use of mean-curvature shading [32].

In [33] we propose another framework for enhancing artifacts. It is based on a definition of a new smooth direction field, termed the *prominent field*, defined for every point on the surface. Intuitively, had the surface been an ideal step edge, this direction would be perpendicular to the ridge, valley, and relief edge.

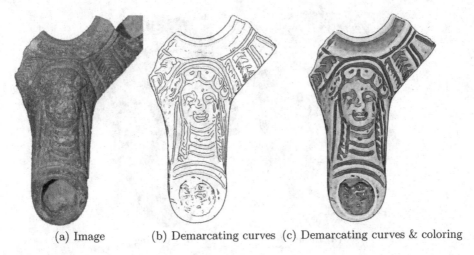

(a) Image   (b) Demarcating curves (c) Demarcating curves & coloring

Fig. 1. A late Hellenistic lamp (150-50 BCE). The lamp is rendered with demarcating curves in (b) and with the addition of coloring in (c).

In practice, however, surfaces are not ideal step edges and thus, we need to define a direction field more carefully.

In essence, for points residing near the ridges and the valleys, the prominent direction should be equal to the first (maximum) principal direction. For points residing near the demarcating edges, the prominent direction should be equal to the relief direction. Since in practice the regions might overlap, these directions are combined as a weighted combination, where the weights are proportional to the likelihood of the point to be near a demarcating curve. Finally, to extend the definition to the whole surface, we search for the smoothest direction field that satisfies the values of the prominent field on the features.

For artificial coloring, the color of a vertex is set according to its curvature in the prominent direction. The lower the curvature, the darker its color. Formally, given a vertex with prominent curvature κ_p, its color is defined as

$$color = \arctan(\lambda \kappa_p),$$

where λ is a user supplied parameter, controlling the overall image contrast.

Figure 2 shows the result of our coloring. It can be seen that this method increases the color contrast on the features, thus enhancing them.

Relief Extraction: Often, we wish to extract the "finger-prints" of an artifact. It is possible to perform this task automatically, when it is known ahead of time that the object at hand is a relief object. These objects are composed of a basic shape or structure and added details. The problem is that the representation of a 3D object as a polygonal mesh, describes both the basic shape and the details with no distinction. This means that important semantic information is missing. Our goal is hence to determine the decoupling of these components, in effect segmenting the object into its base and its details.

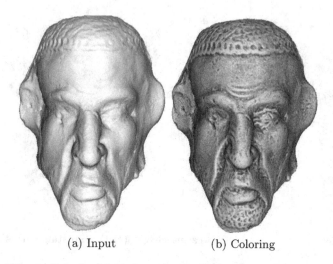

(a) Input   (b) Coloring

Fig. 2. Coloring highlights the subtle features of the object

Our key observation in [34] is that there is no need to extract the real base surface in order to estimate the details. The height function of the details contains all the needed information to separate the relief from the base. Hence, we only need a good estimation of the height and not the base surface itself. Interestingly, this turns out to be easier. We show that to measure height, we only need an estimation of the normals of the base surface, and not the surface itself. Based on the base normals, we can define relative height differences between all the points on the model. By solving a global optimization problem, we eventually reach a height definition for all the points. The reliefs are extracted by thresholding the height function.

Figure 3 illustrates challenging cases, where our algorithm manages to extract the reliefs from noisy and weathered archaeological objects. In such examples both the base and the relief are noisy and the details are lost due to aging.

3   Similarity

After finding a new artifact, the archaeologist aims at locating it in time and space. This is often done manually by leafing through thousands of pages of site reports, where photos and drawings of artifacts are found. This is a Sisyphean procedure, which is extremely time-consuming. Digitizing the findings by a high resolution scanner and creating archaeological databases, which will allow similarity to be expressed as a database query, will be a welcome alternative.

Previous work on matching mainly concentrated on determining the similarity of whole surfaces [1–3]. In the domain of archaeology, however, this does not suffice—we wish to find only similar sub-surfaces, since many artifacts are found broken. The added difficulty stems from the fact that helpful global techniques, such as scaling, alignment, or symmetry cannot be utilized.

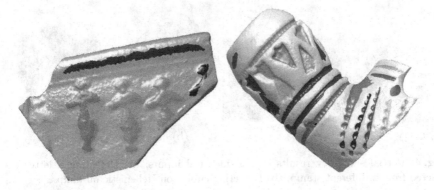

Fig. 3. Examples of relief extraction from a Hellenistic vase (left) and an Ottoman pipe (right)

Therefore, we wish to address *partial similarity*, where given a specific part of an unknown surface, the goal is to detect similar parts on other surfaces, regardless of the global surface this part belongs to.

We propose an algorithm that performs this task [35]. Our key observation is that though isolated feature points often do not suffice, their aggregation provides adequate information regarding similarity. We introduce a probabilistic framework in which segmentation and neighboring feature points allow us to enhance or moderate the certainty of feature similarity.

Specifically, at first, the salient points are detected and their similarity is computed. Considering only a subset of the vertices, rather than the whole set of vertices of the mesh, not only improves the performance, but also enhances the results, since non-distinctive vertices are ignored. Then, the surfaces are segmented into meaningful components and their segments are matched. Next, given the above similarity measures, they are integrated. The goal is to compute consistent correspondences between the salient vertices. Finally, the similar region(s) in one surface is determined according to the correspondence established in the previous stage.

Figure 4 demonstrates the usefulness of our algorithm for the domain of archaeology, in which the data is very noisy, and hence challenging. In particular, in Figure 4(a) the input query is a Greek letter (A) extracted from Hellenistic stamps. Our algorithm manages to detect the letter, even though the letters may differ in shape and the scale ratio is unknown. In Figure 4(b) a cupid from a Hellenistic oil lamp is the query. Our algorithm matches this query to the cupids on a different oil lamp. The poses, as well as the shapes of the matched cupids differ, i.e., the query cupid has hair while the matched cupids do not, the matched cupids have wings while the query does not, etc.

4   Restoration

Restoration refers to bringing back an object to a former condition. In this section we use the term restoration quite liberally, under the goal of conveying some

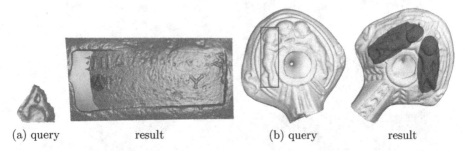

(a) query   result   (b) query   result

Fig. 4. Partial similarity results on non-identical inputs. (a) Detecting a letter extracted from a different stamp. (b) Detecting cupids on Hellenistic oil lamps.

sense of how the artifacts looked like before they were damaged. We focus on three tasks: completion of broken objects in a manner similar to that performed in drawings, reconstruction of a 3D object from its 2D line drawing, and colorization. Other types of restoration, such as pattern restoration, reconstruction of an object from its pieces etc. are left for future work.

Shape Completion: Traditionally, archaeological artifacts are drawn by hand and the artist "completes" the missing data by sketching the major missing feature curves. Our goal is to "complete" the artifacts similarly, albeit in three dimensions. We therefore wish to mathematically define 3D curves, which satisfy several properties, considered to be aesthetic. Furthermore, we devise an algorithm for constructing these curves.

We are inspired by the 2D Euler spirals, which have a long and interesting history. In 1694 Bernoulli wrote the equations for the Euler spirals for the first time. In 1744 Euler rediscovered the curves' equations and described their properties. The curves were rediscovered in 1890 for the third time by Talbot, who used them to design railway tracks. Kimia et al. [36] showed how these spirals can be utilized for 2D curve completion. The characterizing property of these 2D curves is that their curvature evolves linearly along the curve.

In [37] we define the 3D Euler spiral as a curve for which both the curvature and the torsion change linearly with arclength. This property is acknowledged to characterize eye-pleasing curves [38].

We proved that our 3D Euler curves hold the following properties, found to characterize aesthetic curves [39, 40]. They are invariant to similarity transformations; they are symmetric, i.e., the curve leaving the point x_0 with tangent T_0 and reaching the point x_f with tangent T_f coincides with the curve leaving the point x_f with tangent T_f and reaching the point x_0 with tangent T_0; they are extensible; they are smooth; and they are round, i.e., if the curve interpolates two point-tangent pairs lying on a circle, then it is a circle.

Figure 5 demonstrates the use of our spirals for completion in shape illustration. It shows a broken Hellenistic oil lamp, along with curves that would most likely be drawn if the model were complete. These curves are three dimensional and are used jointly with our demarcating curves, described in Section 2.

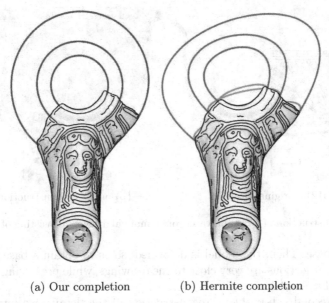

(a) Our completion   (b) Hermite completion

Fig. 5. 3D Euler spirals (red) complete the curves on a broken Hellenistic oil lamp –
curves that would most likely be drawn if the model were complete. They are compared to completion by Hermite-splines. The scale of the Hermite splines is determined
manually (magenta), since the automatically-scaled splines (green) are inferior due to
the large ratio between the length of the curve and the size of the model. Note the
perfect circular arcs of our curves.

Reconstruction from Line Drawing: In some cases, a line drawing of an
artifact, as documented in the site report, is the only available source of information. Our goal is to reconstruct a surface, given a line drawing of a relief
object. Automatic reconstruction from a line drawing is a challenging task due
to several reasons. First, the lines are usually sparse and thus, the object is
not fully constrained by the input. Second, the lines are often ambiguous, since
they may have different geometric meanings—they can indicate 3D discontinuities, surface creases, or 3D step edges. Third, the input may consist of a large
number of strokes that need to be handled by the algorithm efficiently. Fourth,
these strokes are inter-related. For instance, the decorations may be either pro-
truded or indented as a whole, and a solution in which some of the lines indicate
protrusions and others indentations is less likely.

In [41] we propose a solution to the problem. We divide this problem into two
sub-problems: reconstruction of the base and reconstruction of the details (i.e.
the relief) on top of the base. We address each of them separately, as follows.

For the base, since the drawing in under-constrained, we pursue a data-
driven approach, which is able to reconstruct highly complex bases. As available
databases are not guaranteed to contain a model that accurately fits the line
drawings' outline, the retrieved base has to be modified. Hence, our algorithm
consists of two stages. First, given the drawings, it finds the most similar model

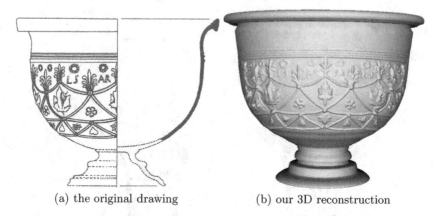

(a) the original drawing   (b) our 3D reconstruction

Fig. 6. Reconstruction of a Roman vase from a manual drawing consisting of 571 curves

in the database. Then, the model is deformed, so as to obtain a base whose orthographic projections are very close to the drawings, while preserving the shape of the matched model.

For the second sub-problem, reconstruction of the details, we introduce an algorithm for generating the relief on a given base. We assume that the details can be described as a height function defined on the base and that the lines of drawings of relief objects indicate changes of the height function. Therefore, we want to compute the relief object, such that near the curves the shape of the cross section matches the shape of a 3D step edge, whereas elsewhere its shape is smooth and similar to the base. Specifically, we need to compute the height for the step edge of every curve in a consistent manner. The key idea of our method is to reduce the problem of restoring the height of every step edge to the problem of constrained topological ordering of a graph. Once the relief is defined locally, in the curves' neighborhood, we need to reconstruct the rest of the mesh. We do it globally, by defining the relief as the smoothest function that coincides with the relief obtained locally for every curve.

Figure 6 shows the reconstruction of an intricate relief of a vase. Though the drawing consists of 571 tightly interconnected lines, the reconstruction achieves visually-pleasing results.

Colorization: Colorization traditionally refers to the computer-assisted process for adding color to black-and-white images and movies. For 3D models, colorization has hardly been explored. Instead, models are usually textured by images. There are, however, applications that do not need rich textures, but rather require colorization by just a handful of colors. For such applications, texture mapping is not only an overkill, but it might also produce incorrect output. More importantly, it requires an image that is similar to the model and contains the right texture—an image that does not necessarily exist. Archaeology is such an application.

Specifically, the common perception of the great statues and buildings of ancient Greece and Rome is that they were all pure unpainted stone or green tarnished bronze. However, lately researchers have been arguing that these statues were quite alive, vibrant, and full of color [42]. Unfortunately, after centuries of deterioration any trace of pigment leftover when discovered, would have been taken off during the cleaning processes done before being put on display. Researchers argue that the number of colors and hues used by the artists was limited. In addition, chemical analysis can often estimate the original color. In this case, colorization algorithms will be able to restore the look of the scanned statues.

We propose a novel mesh colorization algorithm [43], which can restore the look of such scanned statues. It does not require mesh segmentation, which often fails to correctly identify complex region boundaries. Our algorithm is inspired by the image colorization algorithm of [44]. There, the user can scribble some desired colors in the interiors of various regions of the image. Colorization is then formulated as a constrained quadratic optimization problem, where the basic assumption is that adjacent pixels having similar intensities should have similar colors

The extension to meshes is not straightforward, due to two issues. First, a fundamental assumption in images is that the work is performed in the YUV color space, and that the intensity Y is given. To determine whether two neighboring pixels should be colorized using the same color, their intensities are compared. In the case of meshes, the intensity channel does not exist. Therefore, a different technique is needed for determining whether neighboring points should be colorized similarly. Second, a limitation of [44] is that colors may bleed into each other. This is fixed in subsequent papers, by applying edge detection that bounds the regions [45]. On meshes, however, existing edge detection algorithms often generate broken curves, through which colors can bleed.

Our algorithm handles these challenges [43]. The key idea is that nearby vertices with similar geometry should get the same color. We thus present a vertex similarity measure that can be used to determine whether two vertices should get the same color. Based on this similarity, we formulate an optimization problem that can be solved efficiently. Moreover, we introduce a new direction field on meshes. We show how the optimization problem can be modified using our direction field, so as to prevent bleeding despite the fact that surface edges are broken.

To colorize a model, the user scribbles the desired colors on the mesh. For each face the scribble passes through, the closest vertex is colorized with the color of the scribble. These colored vertices are considered the user defined constraints. The algorithm then automatically propagates the colors to the remaining vertices of the mesh in two steps. First, a similarity measure between neighboring vertices is computed and assigned to the corresponding edges. This similarity is based on our variation of spin images [46]. Then, given the scribbles and the above similarities, the colors are propagated to the whole mesh. The optimization attempts to minimize the difference between the color at a vertex and the weighted average of the colors at neighboring vertices, where the weight is large

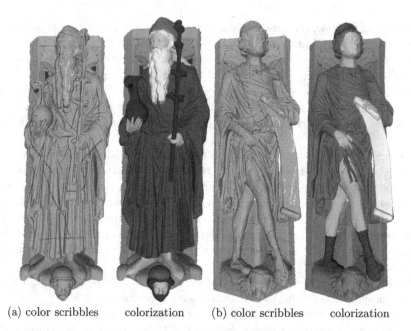

(a) color scribbles   colorization   (b) color scribbles   colorization

Fig. 7. Only a few scribbles are needed to colorize the cloth, despite its folded structure. Note how the fingers are separated from the folded cloth or the hand-held objects.

when the descriptors are similar. The output is a mesh in which every vertex has a designated color.

Figure 7 shows a couple of examples where convincing results are generated by our algorithm, given a small number of color scribbles. Note how our algorithm manages to distinguish between the individual fingers and the cloth or the other hand-held objects. Moreover, despite the multiple folds of the cloth, it is easily colored using only a few scribbles that cross it.

5   Summary

A lot of progress has been recently made in shape analysis in computer graphics. However, little of this progress has had a profound influence on archaeology. In this paper we describe our work, performed in the last several years, whose goal is expose the progress in shape analysis to the domain of archaeology. We believe that the mutual interaction of these areas has to potential to impact both fields. In computer graphics, algorithms for solving fundamental problems, such as completion, reconstruction, and matching, which manage to handle the complex archaeological data, will expose the limits of the current techniques. Hence, new algorithms developed for this domain are likely to advance the state-of-the-art. In archaeology, automation may transform the way archaeologists work. Computerized techniques and tools will enable the archaeologist to process the findings immediately and automatically. It is required that the artifacts are scanned by a 3D scanner and represented as polygonal meshes—no metadata or semantics are being used.

We view our work as part of a world-wide effort to overcome the difficulties and enable fast, accurate, and user-friendly analysis of archaeological artifact. In this paper we present several works. In particular, in the section on documentation we describe 3D display by feature curves, by black & white coloring, and by relief extraction. In the section on similarity, we introduce an algorithm for detecting partial matches. In the section on restoration, we discuss shape completion, reconstruction of an object from its line drawing, and virtual colorization. Our data is available for academic research purposes.

Acknowledgements. First and foremost, I would like to thank my students, who participated in this research: Gur Harary, Arik Itskovich, Michael Kolomenkin, George Leifman, and Rony Zatzarinni. I would like to thank Ayellet Gilboa and the Zinman Institute of Archaeology at the University of Haifa and Ilan Shimshoni for their collaboration in this research. Finally, this research was supported in part by the Israel Science Foundation (ISF) 1420/12, the Argentinian Research Fund, and the Ollendorff foundation.

References

1. van Kaick, O., Zhang, H., Hamarneh, G., Cohen-Or, D.: A survey on shape correspondence. In: Proc. of Eurographics State-of-the-art Report (2010)
2. Tangelder, J., Veltkamp, R.: A survey of content based 3D shape retrieval methods. Multimedia Tools and Applications 39(3), 441–471 (2008)
3. Leifman, G., Meir, R., Tal, A.: Semantic-oriented 3D shape retrieval using relevance feedback. The Visual Computer (Pacific Graphics) 21(8-10), 865–875 (2005)
4. Attene, M., Katz, S., Mortara, M., Patané, G., Spagnuolo, M., Tal, A.: Mesh segmentation-a comparative study. In: Shape Modeling and Applications (2006)
5. Katz, S., Tal, A.: Hierarchical mesh decomposition using fuzzy clustering and cuts. ACM Trans. Graph. 22(3), 954–961 (2003)
6. Shamir, A.: A survey on mesh segmentation techniques. Computer Graphics Forum 27, 1539–1556 (2008)
7. Besl, P., McKay, H.: A method for registration of 3-D shapes. IEEE Trans. on Pattern Analysis and Machine Intelligence 14(2), 239–256 (1992)
8. Lucas, B., Kanade, T., et al.: An iterative image registration technique with an application to stereo vision. In: 7th International Joint Conference on Artificial Intelligence (1981)
9. DeCarlo, D., Finkelstein, A., Rusinkiewicz, S., Santella, A.: Suggestive contours for conveying shape. ACM Transactions on Graphics 22(3), 848–855 (2003)
10. Judd, T., Durand, F., Adelson, E.: Apparent ridges for line drawing. ACM Transactions on Graphics 26(3), 19:1–19:7 (2007)
11. Ohtake, Y., Belyaev, A., Seidel, H.: Ridge-valley lines on meshes via implicit surface fitting. ACM Transactions on Graphics 23(3), 609–612 (2004)
12. Lee, C., Varshney, A., Jacobs, D.: Mesh saliency. ACM Trans. on Graph. 24(3), 659–666 (2005)

13. Shilane, P., Funkhouser, T.: Distinctive regions of 3D surfaces. ACM Trans. on Graphics 26(2) (2007)
14. Leifman, G., Shtrom, E., Tal, A.: Surface regions of interest for viewpoint selection. In: IEEE Computer Vision and Pattern Recognition (CVPR), pp. 414–421 (2012)
15. Ju, T.: Fixing geometric errors on polygonal models: a survey. J. of Computer Science and Technology 24(1), 19–29 (2009)
16. Liepa, P.: Filling holes in meshes. In: SGP, pp. 200–205 (2003)
17. Sharf, A., Alexa, M., Cohen-Or, D.: Context-based surface completion. ACM Transactions on Graphics 23(3), 878–887 (2004)
18. Levoy, M., Pulli, K., Curless, B., Rusinkiewicz, R., Koller, D., Pereira, L., Ginzton, M., Anderson, S., Davis, J., Ginsberg, J., Shade, J., Fulk, D.: The digital michelangelo project: 3D scanning of large statues. In: Proceedings of ACM SIGGRAPH 2000, pp. 131–144 (July 2000)
19. Brown, B., Toler-Franklin, C., Nehab, D., Burns, M., Dobkin, D., Vlachopoulos, A., Doumas, C., Rusinkiewicz, S., Weyric, T.: A system for high-volume acquisition and matching of fresco fragments: Reassembling Theran wall paintings. ACM Trans. Graph. 27(3), 84:1–84:9 (2008)
20. Gilboa, A., Tal, A., Shimshoni, I., Kolomenkin, M.: Computer-based, automatic recording and illustration of complex archaeological artifacts. Journal of Archaeological Science (2012)
21. Cignoni, P., Scopigno, R.: Sampled 3d models for ch applications: A viable and enabling new medium or just a technological exercise? Journal on Computing and Cultural Heritage 1(1) (2008)
22. Brutto, M., Spera, M.: Image-based and range-based 3D modeling of archaeological cultural heritage: the Telamon of the Temple of Olympian Zeus in Agrigento (Italy). In: International Archives of Photogrammetry, Remote Sensing and Spatial Information Sciences (2011)
23. Gilboa, A., Karasik, A., Sharon, I., Smilansky, U.: Computerized typology and classification of ceramics. Journal of Archaeological Science 31, 681–694 (2004)
24. Hanke, K., Moser, M., Grimm-Pitzinger, A., Goldenberg, G., Toechterle, U.: Enhanced potential for the analysis of archaeological finds based on 3d modeling. In: The International Archives of the Photogrammetry, Remote Sensing and Spatial Information Sciences XXXVII, Part B, vol. 5, pp. 187–192 (2008)
25. Karasik, A., Smilansky, U.: 3D scanning technology as a standard archaeological tool for pottery analysis: practice and theory. Journal of Archaeological Science 35 (2008)
26. Pires, H., Ortiz, P., Marques, P., Sanchez, H.: Close-range laser scanning applied to archaeological artifacts documentation. In: International Symposium on Virtual Reality, Archaeology and Cultural Heritage (VAST), pp. 284–289 (2006)
27. Gooch, B., Gooch, A.: Non-Photorealistic Rendering. AK Peters Ltd. (2001)
28. Biederman, I.: Visual Cognition. MIT Press, Cambridge, MA and London (1995)
29. Kolomenkin, M., Shimshoni, I., Tal, A.: Demarcating curves for shape illustration. ACM Transactions on Graphics 27(5), 157:1–157:9 (2008)
30. Kolomenkin, M., Shimshoni, I., Tal, A.: On edge detection on surfaces. In: CVPR, pp. 2767–2774 (2009)
31. Ohtake, Y., Belyaev, A., Seidel, H.P.: Ridge-valley lines on meshes via implicit surface fitting. ACM Trans. Graph. 23(3), 609–612 (2004)
32. Kindlmann, G., Whitaker, R., Tasdizen, T., Moller, T.: Curvature-Based Transfer Functions for Direct Volume Rendering: Methods and Applications. In: IEEE Visualization, pp. 67–76 (2003)

33. Kolomenkin, M., Shimshoni, I., Tal, A.: Prominent field for shape processing of archaeological artifacts. IJCV 94(1), 89–100 (2011)
34. Zatzarinni, R., Tal, A., Shamir, A.: Relief analysis and extraction. ACM Transactions on Graphics 28(5), 136 (2009)
35. Itskovich, A., Tal, A.: Surface partial matching and application to archaeology. Computers & Graphics (2011)
36. Kimia, B., Frankel, I., Popescu, A.: Euler spiral for shape completion. Int. J. Comp. Vision 54(1), 159–182 (2003)
37. Harary, G., Tal, A.: 3D Euler spirals for 3D curve completion. Computational Geometry: Theory and Applications 45(3), 115–126 (2012)
38. Singh, M., Fulvio, J.: Visual extrapolation of contour geometry. PNAS 102(3), 939–944 (2005)
39. Knuth, D.: Mathematical typography. Bulletin AMS 1(2), 337–372 (1979)
40. Ullman, S.: Filling-in the gaps: The shape of subjective contours and a model for their generation. Biological Cybernetics 25(1), 1–6 (1976)
41. Kolomenkin, M., Leifman, G., Shimshoni, I., Tal, A.: Reconstruction of relief objects from line drawings. CVPR 2(12), 13–19 (2011)
42. Bonn-Muller, E.: Carved in living color. Archaeology 61(1) (2008)
43. Leifman, G., Tal, A.: Mesh colorization. Computer Graphics Forum 31(2), 421–430 (2012)
44. Levin, A., Lischinski, D., Weiss, Y.: Colorization using optimization. ACM Transactions on Graphics 23(3), 689–694 (2004)
45. Huang, Y.C., Tung, Y.S., Chen, J.C., Wang, S.W., Wu, J.L.: An adaptive edge detection based colorization algorithm and its applications. ACM Multimedia, 351–354 (2005)
46. Johnson, A., Hebert, M.: Using spin images for efficient object recognition in cluttered 3D scenes. IEEE Trans. Pattern Anal. Mach. Intell. 21(5), 433–449 (1999)

Procedural Shape Modeling in Digital Humanities: Potentials and Issues

Sven Havemann[1], Olaf Wagener[3], and Dieter Fellner[1,2]

[1] Institute of Computer Graphics and Knowledge Visualization,
Graz University of Technology, Austria
[2] Fraunhofer IGD and TU Darmstadt, Germany
[3] Institut für Europäische Kunstgeschichte, University of Heidelberg, Germany
{s.havemann,d.fellner}@cgv.tugraz.at, olaf.wagener@gmx.de

Abstract. Procedural modeling is a technology that has great potential to make the abundant variety of shapes that have to be dealt with in Digital Humanities accessible and understandable. There is a gap, however, between technology on the one hand and the needs and requirements of the users in the Humanities community. In this paper we analyze the reasons for the limited uptake of procedural modeling and sketch possible ways to circumvent the problem. The key insight is that we have to find matching concepts in both fields, which are on the one hand grounded in the way shape is explained, e.g., in art history, but which can also be formalized to make them accessible to digital computers.

Keywords: Shape modeling, 3D-reconstruction, procedural modeling, digital humanities, shape understanding, domain-specific languages.

1 Introduction

Currently there is much discussion about the mission of the evolving field *Digital Humanities*. We believe this concept can potentially deliver both a broader and a more targeted view on the research field previously known as *ICT for Cultural Heritage* (CH). The latter has produced a range of CH-adapted technologies in various research projects, only to mention large-scale initiatives such as the projects EPOCH (EU FP6 network of excellence) [1] and 3D-COFORM (EU FP7 Integrated Project) [2,3,4]. Today technologies are available for 3D-acquisition and processing, for 3D-searching, internet delivery and photo-realistic interactive presentation, but also semantic technologies for describing provenance and authenticity of 3D datasets. Furthermore, empirically grounded ontology standards such as CIDOC-CRM [5] are capable of expressing a wide range of cultural facts that can be stored in semantic networks that may grow ever denser over time. The big question is, where does all this lead to – and what is it good for?

While ICT for CH is mostly technology driven, Digital Humanities come from the other side, so to speak: The emphasis is on *Humanities*. It seems, though, that a major effort is required for bridging the gap between the disciplines: Engineering focuses on measurable quantitative objectives, and on developing new approaches and methods;

M. Ioannides and E. Quak (Eds.): 3D Research Challenges, LNCS 8355, pp. 64–77, 2014.

the scientific community favors fast review cycles with peer-reviewed journals and conferences. Humanities focus on qualitative interpretations; often there is no single truth, and different and even contradicting schools may co-exist; the scientific community values books and monographs that are thoroughly prepared.

We have realized that for finding a common ground for collaboration, a working assumption is very useful as a smallest common denominator to join both disciplines:

Assumption 1: The purpose of any scientific work is to explain the real world.

The specific topic of this paper is the treatment of shape, which is of particular interest in art history. A major observation is that there are two fundamentally different views on shape, we call it the *documentary* and the *conceptual* view. A hypothetic example may be the remains of a destroyed rounded stone arch. The documentation problem is solved by collecting the facts[1] , i.e., by 3D scanning the site and the individual stones. With the aid of computer graphics the arch can be virtually reconstructed once it is clear where each stone is to be placed (3D puzzle problem).

Nowhere in this reconstruction, however, appears the radius of the arch explicitly. And without a common concept of a "round arch" this reconstruction cannot even be related to other reconstructions of round arches. Thus, the more abstract, interpretative conceptual view is indispensable for explaining the arch (see Assumption 1 above), which is true in art history as well as in archeology.

Assumption 2: Digital Humanities depart from documentation (facts) to produce interpretations (meaning), obtaining conceptual views from documentary views.

We have observed that although in Humanities, research can mean to produce an extensive description of a single iconic cultural artifact (e.g., a vase) there is still the desire to produce more general explanations of real world phenomena, especially of the past. The dilemma, however, is that understanding and explaining are tasks that are inherently manual, and thus, do not scale. Scalability is an issue because of the richness and diversity of the real world: the number of researchers and the amount of facts are very unbalanced. To give one example, the estimated number of castles in the three countries Germany, Austria and Swiss is about 30.000, versus a few hundred castle researchers in these countries; and castles can be very complex as they typically vary substantially over time, and thus, they are difficult to explain.

Assumption 3: Research in Humanities is affected by limited scalability.

We think that once the knowledge (explanations, interpretations) is produced, another important need is to improve the interoperability of research results in the Humanities. Various initiatives aim at making research results from the Humanities accessible via internet, only to mention the long lists of projects at ZIM in Graz [6]

---

[1] A noteworthy subtlety is that when speaking about facts in this context, we always mean raw measurements. Not a statue is considered a fact, but the color of the pixel of the photograph of the statue, from a measurement taken at a specific time under specific illumination.

and at CCeH in Cologne [7]. The problem, though, is the vertical structure of these projects and the limited horizontal interconnectedness; it is difficult to access one project from another, as much as it is difficult to relate one monograph on castles, or vases, to another monograph in the same field treating a different artifact. This can be solved by identifying common underlying concepts, as was demonstrated by the CIDOC CRM which uses only five core concepts to express most cultural facts: actor, event, place, time, thing. This simplicity is the result of a compactification process over ten years. Today (in version 5.1) only 90 entity and 152 property (relation) types are sufficient to achieve sufficient expressiveness for formalizing cultural facts.

Assumption 4: A small, standardized vocabulary of common concepts is the precondition for scalability and for interoperability.

This leads to the question: **What is the equivalent of an *adequate vocabulary* for shape?** In order to approach the problem we will first look at how art historians work, our chosen example discipline in Digital Humanities. This is followed by a discourse on procedural modeling and a demonstration of its explanatory power in an example use case. This finally leads to some serious issues that require targeted research.

2   Supporting Shape-Related Research in Art History

Interpreting and reasoning about the shape of objects of historical significance is an important part of art historical research. Art historians structure, classify, explain, and relate existing artifacts, and resort to educated speculation when they need to deal with uncertainty and incomplete information. Although scientific thinking and understanding of many art historians is genuinely three-dimensional, the traditional way of communication is exclusively 2D. In art historical publications, shape is described using plans, sections, and orthogonal views (see Figure 1). This is in many cases the appropriate level of abstraction for the discourse; but in many cases it is not. Returning to the example of castles, 3D is indispensable because castles are multi-purpose buildings that can be understood only in their entirety, considering for example their appearance, their perception, and their topographic relations. 2D plans are simply not sufficient to describe unambiguously the three-dimensional shape of a castle. The unavoidable loss of information impedes the scientific discourse because accurate reasoning about function or significance of details of a historic building is possible only when taking into account the 3D ensemble. Holistic analyses require precise spatial relations, possibly including even visibility and lighting.

Assuming the goal of research in Humanities is to produce interpretations of evidence (documented facts), the fundamental question is whether and how computer based methods (especially 3D) can support this work. We suggest the following areas:

- **Formalization:** Shape can typically be decomposed into sub-parts that are distinguishable and meaningful (staircase $\rightarrow$ stair) until arriving at the "smallest meaningful parts", (building $\rightarrow$ stone). A digital description of the parts and their connections can yield different *conceptual views* of the shape.

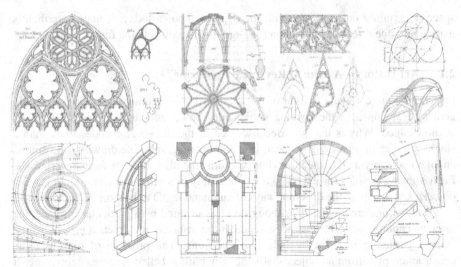

Fig. 1. Historical illustrations of complex constructions from different books. Note the different ways to convey three-dimensionality. Also note the explanatory power of the abstractions, and that each is well-chosen to be variable and generalizable.

- **Construction system:** The part-whole relationship is an interpretation, and it is not unique. But any decomposition into parts yields also a construction system, since the parts can be understood as re-usable shape building blocks.

- **Variability**: To deal with incomplete or missing information, art historians try out different alternative 3D reconstruction hypotheses, use different sets of construction elements and different decomposition schemas, and discuss them. This is a genuine part of the scientific work of art historians.

- **Canonical decomposition:** Given a set of shape building blocks and a shape to decompose, it is desirable that different experts shall obtain very similar, if not identical, decompositions (and thus, formal descriptions). If it exists, we call this the "canonical" decomposition of the shape into sub-shapes of the set.

- **Fitness for purpose:** There is no such thing as *the* only true 3D-reconstruction of a real object. For a 3D-reconstruction to be of scientific value it must allow deriving sound scientific conclusions. So the *fitness for a purpose* of a 3D-reconstruction depends on the questions that need to be answered.

In combination, these features would enable a new form of scientific discourse in many areas of art historical research. A 3D reconstruction is as much the result of scientific work as it also inspires examining new questions. A scientifically validated 3D reference model (e.g., of a castle or a vase) could evolve to an ***integrated knowledge space*** through annotations and linking to photographs, remarks, legacy texts, restoration reports, and so on – a 3D reconstruction could ultimately lead to a whole semantic network of facts and findings. Although the integrated knowledge space is certainly out of scope with the methods known today, it may nevertheless mark a possible direction and vision for Digital Humanities in the future.

2.1   Art History – A form of Reverse Engineering?

Inspecting Figure 1 again in light of Assumption 1 – explaining the world is the main goal of Humanities – the striking explanatory power of these drawings has to be acknowledged. Why is that so? Because each of the drawings encodes more than a single instance of a particular object; it is not a photograph. The drawings are simple enough to convey a clear meaning, but each drawing also suggests various variations. Each drawing denotes (or encodes) a whole family of similar drawings, and even 3D objects; and also note the different ways of augmenting 2D to become 3D.

The drawings are idealized. Although each is inspired by a particular instance, the drawing captures only the abstract essence of the instance; it extracts a general recipe from a particular instance by inductive reasoning. The problem of obtaining the construction plan from an object that is already built is called *reverse engineering*. It is an inverse problem that is conceptually more difficult than the forward problem, namely following a plan step by step to produce an object.

But if these drawings are good in explaining, what is their digital equivalent?

3   Procedural Shape Modeling and Its Uptake in Art History

For its many virtues, the parametric description of shape has been rapidly adopted in industrial design and manufacturing since the 1990s: Parametric norm-parts can easily be adjusted to fit by changing a few high-level parameters, model changes can be quickly accommodated, and the re-usability of parametric parts is obviously much higher. Additional advantages are compact model sizes and improved scalability: Modern flavors of parametrics include generative and procedural approaches, where huge geometric models are generated based on rules and procedures, even to the point of generating whole cities. So it is a solution to the scalability problem.

We argue that procedural and generative shape descriptions are a perfect match for Digital Humanities. History is rich and diverse, and obtaining an accurate, integrated understanding requires recreating the historical surroundings in great detail; this is where scalability is important. Manually modeling the past is simply not feasible.

Even more important, though, may be an aspect that is commonly seen as a disadvantage: Creating procedural models is not possible without *understanding*. The shape parameters of a Greek temple are intricately interrelated based on laws of proportion, so that there are only surprisingly few effective degrees of freedom; most parameters are in fact dependent variables. This shows the potential value of parametric and procedural shape descriptions. The documentary view (3D-scanning) requires no understanding, but it also delivers no understanding. Only when complemented by a conceptual view, both aspects of work in the Humanities are covered: Faithful documentation of facts, and meaningful interpretation.

We advocate the use of generative shape descriptions as a research tool in Digital Humanities. They should be proposed, exchanged, and argued about by researchers. Shape knowledge can be accumulated in procedural style libraries to make it sustainable, for understanding and explaining the past, for searching and browsing. The question remaining is: What are the obstacles impeding its further proliferation, and why is this technology not yet used to the degree possible?

3.1 Related Work on Procedural 3D Reconstructions in Cultural Heritage

Various authors have in fact pursued the idea of using procedural 3D modeling techniques for 3D reconstructions in Cultural Heritage. The technologies employed are very diverse. One prominent early cluster of technologies is related to shape grammars, which were introduced as early as 1971 by Stiny and Mitchell. They were able to explain the structure of Palladian villas using the principle of recursive refinement [8]. The principle is simple and general: A (context free) grammar rule specifies how a single labeled shape (scope) is replaced by a set of smaller shapes with other labels. This fits well with the top-down approach in classical architecture, e.g. for the recreation of Frank Lloyd Wright's prairie houses by Koning et al. [9], the bungalows of Buffalo by Downing et al. [10], Queen Anne houses by Flemming [11], Christopher Wren's city churches by Buelinckx [12], and Alvaro Siza's houses at Malagueira by Duarte [13,14]. Duarte et al. also used shape grammars to describe the more irregular structure of the city Medina of Marrakech [15].

A new take on the problem was proposed by Müller et al. who introduced split grammars as a specialization of shape grammars: Their scopes are not arbitrary shapes but axis-aligned boxes that can be split into smaller boxes along the principal axes using subdivide and repeat operators. They demonstrated the feasibility of their approach by city-scale reconstructions, e.g., of the Maya architecture in Xkipche [16] and with the famous Rome Reborn 2.0 project [17]. Despite these excellent case studies the uptake of the approach in the Humanities community is limited. Writing grammar rules is similar to programming, and the effort apparently does not match up with the results. A conceptual problem with recursive replacement is that it works strictly in a top-down fashion so that many dependencies cannot be expressed; in other words, the explanatory power is limited.

Other authors therefore resorted to professional parametric CAD software, e.g., Fassi and Parri who obtained impressive results with a part of Milan cathedral [18]. The parametric approach conveys a deep understanding of the construction; unfortunately, it is only accessible to CAD experts.

A very interesting middle ground that is also accessible to the Heritage community was found by De Luca et al. [19] who decomposed classical architecture into meaningful parametric components that can be described by sections and drawings (see Figure 1); their software allows interactive composition and editing of the parts.

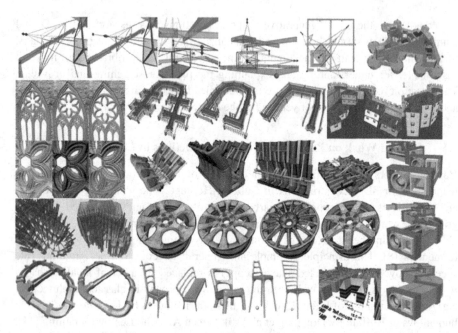

Fig. 2. GML models encode not only a single shape, but a whole shape family

The approaches developed in our group use a programming language for shape, the *Generative Modeling Language* (GML) with its OpenGL-based runtime engine [20] (Fig. 2). The construction of a shape is encoded as a sequence of tokens that either contain data, which are pushed on a stack, or processing instructions (operators), which are executed. The concept is simple and powerful; GML was used to describe Gothic window tracery [21], an interactive modeler for castles [22], shape grammars [23], and for the interactive composition of parametric shapes [24]; for an overview see [25]. However, writing GML programs is not suitable for art historians. Can GML still help in making procedural (generative) modeling useful and usable for them?

4   Case Study: Understanding Neo-Classical Windows

The examples in the previous section show that procedural technology is well suited for Cultural Heritage, and the question is why it is not used more. We have come to the conclusion that the problem is less technology, but more how to organize the process of knowledge aggregation and accumulation. The research focus should shift towards finding methods for *developing* procedural models in a structured way.

The crucial question then is how to adapt procedural shape modeling to the concepts used in the target audience, art historians and Humanities researchers. We believe a bridge can be derived from Figure 1: The constructions shown are both accessible to art historians, and they can also be formalized. The variability in these drawings, however, is only implicit and not explicit, i.e., they do not offer parameters to change. So this is the message to be delivered: The understanding of such

Fig. 3. Exemplars to be understood and explained, from 120 in total

'variable' drawings must be described in a 'variable' way. In technical terms: Procedural shapes deserve a procedural representation.

As a bridge in between, and as means of communication, we propose *domain-specific languages*. Technically, these are light-weight programming languages with operations adapted to the domain. From the point of view of art historians, they are cooking recipes for shape; so each of the drawings in Figure 1 must be translated to a sequence of operations. But how can this be carried out in practice? We summarize the method presented in [26] with respect to solving this problem.

4.1   Reverse Engineering of Neo-Classical Windows

The process starts with a certain number of given exemplars spanning a shape space. The exemplars in this case are 120 images of windows in neo-classical facades in Graz, Austria (Figure 3). The typical approach of art historians to describing window styles is by classification. We propose exactly the same, but with a slight extension: The classification must be 'executable'. The process starts as follows:

Fact Labeling Method
- Exemplars are treated as *facts*
- Each fact is associated with *observations*
- Similar observations are grouped
- Observations can be mutually exclusive, i.e., *alternatives*
    - A window may be round or rectangular, but not both
- *Label group*: Set of Alternatives with *group labels* A, B, C, ...
- *Labels* A1, A2, A3, ... are assigned to each of the alternatives

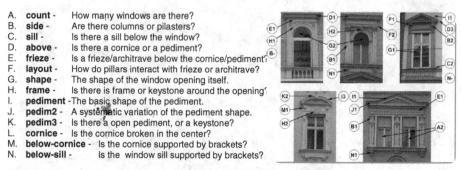

A. **count** - How many windows are there?
B. **side** - Are there columns or pilasters?
C. **sill** - Is there a sill below the window?
D. **above** - Is there a cornice or a pediment?
E. **frieze** - Is a frieze/architrave below the cornice/pediment?
F. **layout** - How do pillars interact with frieze or architrave?
G. **shape** - The shape of the window opening itself.
H. **frame** - Is there is frame or keystone around the opening?
I. **pediment** - The basic shape of the pediment.
J. **pedim2** - A systematic variation of the pediment shape.
K. **pedim3** - Is there a open pediment, or a keystone?
L. **cornice** - Is the cornice broken in the center?
M. **below-cornice** - Is the cornice supported by brackets?
N. **below-sill** - Is the window sill supported by brackets?

Fig. 4. Observations can be formulated as labeled questions that are answered for each exemplar, if applicable; but sometimes the questions must be reformulated

Note that this is only a reformulation in engineering terms of a well established method; we claim that *any* classification process in art history or archeology has to proceed in such a way (maybe without the labels). So we assume that this method is easy to grasp by Humanities researchers (see Fig. 4). In order to encode the variability of shapes, however, this method has to be embedded in an iterative process:

Generative Fact Labeling (GFL) Method

1. *Analysis Phase*
   Fact labeling step: Create / refine observations, alternatives, labels
2. *Synthesis Phase*
   Shape programming step: Create / refine a library of procedural assets
3. *Verification Phase*:   Can all observations be reproduced?
4. *Iterative Optimization*:   Back to step 1.

The iterative optimization (step 4) is tedious but indispensable. Among the 120 windows there are so many variants that once it seems that a rule is found, there is often also a counter-example. The usual solution in such cases is to subdivide larger observations into smaller ones, which leads to *re-labeling*. The decomposition of a shape into "smallest meaningful parts" eventually leads to elementary procedural shape building blocks that can be combined to re-generate the exemplars. Note that in software engineering, this process is called *refactoring*.

The classifications that are produced in this fashion differ in important respects from those in art history, because the focus is exclusively on grouping together shape variations by *shape similarity*. The discussion with a domain specialist – Prof. Hain from the institute of building history at TU Graz – revealed an important difference to their work, namely that socio-historical context and high-level stylistic influences are more in their focus than just shape. They strive for a much more comprehensive and holistic understanding of a building and see it in its whole complexity; the *gestalt* of a façade, for instance, can immediately tell the specialist that the builder was a freemason. The positive experience, however, was that the specialists indeed do possess detailed shape knowledge, and that the generative classification we obtained matches to a large extent with the established architectural vocabulary (c.f. Fig. 4).

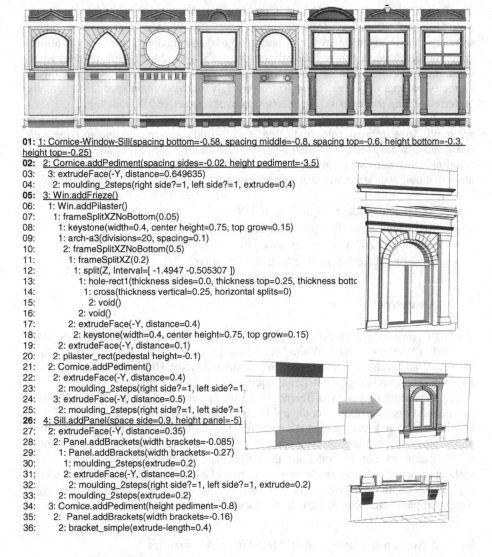

```
01: 1: Cornice-Window-Sill(spacing bottom=-0.58, spacing middle=-0.8, spacing top=-0.6, height bottom=-0.3,
    height top=-0.25)
02: 2: Cornice.addPediment(spacing sides=-0.02, height pediment=-3.5)
03:    3: extrudeFace(-Y, distance=0.649635)
04:    2: moulding_2steps(right side?=1, left side?=1, extrude=0.4)
05: 3: Win.addFrieze()
06:    1: Win.addPilaster()
07:    1: frameSplitXZNoBottom(0.05)
08:    1: keystone(width=0.4, center height=0.75, top grow=0.15)
09:    1: arch-a3(divisions=20, spacing=0.1)
10:       2: frameSplitXZNoBottom(0.5)
11:          1: frameSplitXZ(0.2)
12:             1: split(Z, Interval=[ -1.4947 -0.505307 ])
13:                1: hole-rect1(thickness sides=0.0, thickness top=0.25, thickness bottc
14:                   1: cross(thickness vertical=0.25, horizontal splits=0)
15:                      2: void()
16:                2: void()
17:       2: extrudeFace(-Y, distance=0.4)
18:          2: keystone(width=0.4, center height=0.75, top grow=0.15)
19:    2: extrudeFace(-Y, distance=0.1)
20:    2: pilaster_rect(pedestal height=-0.1)
21:    2: Cornice.addPediment()
22:       2: extrudeFace(-Y, distance=0.4)
23:       2: moulding_2steps(right side?=1, left side?=1,
24:    3: extrudeFace(-Y, distance=0.5)
25:       2: moulding_2steps(right side?=1, left side?=1
26: 4: Sill.addPanel(space side=0.9, height panel=-5)
27:    2: extrudeFace(-Y, distance=0.35)
28:       2: Panel.addBrackets(width brackets=-0.085)
29:          1: Panel.addBrackets(width brackets=-0.27)
30:             1: moulding_2steps(extrude=0.2)
31:          2: extrudeFace(-Y, distance=0.2)
32:             2: moulding_2steps(right side?=1, left side?=1, extrude=0.2)
33:          2: moulding_2steps(extrude=0.2)
34:    3: Cornice.addPediment(height pediment=-0.8)
35:       2: Panel.addBrackets(width brackets=-0.16)
36:          2: bracket_simple(extrude-length=0.4)
```

Fig. 5. Description of a window using a tree of domain-specific operations. Operations that are indented operate on geometry produced by previous operations. Top: Geometry produced by the different domain-specific shape operations.

4.2   Results and Limitations

One very satisfying result of this exercise was that it is indeed much faster to reconstruct a particular window when a similar window is already reconstructed, the description of which can be edited, than reconstructing a window from scratch (see Fig. 6). With a bit of experience it is indeed possible also for domain specialists to directly edit the window description in the domain specific language shown in Fig. 5. Based on the technology from [24] we have also created interactive modeling software that is extensible with respect to the shape modeling tools, so it allows applying the shape operations directly on the 3D shapes. Much work remains to be done, though, to facilitate the interactive editing process of procedural shapes; this is currently an area of active research. Surprisingly, some domain specialists actually preferred editing the textual code description over interactive 3D modeling.

The limits of the classification process, however, became clear as well: Architects apparently love to break rules and often need to find creative solutions to cope with constraints. In case there is not enough room for all elements, for example, often the solution is to intertwine elements that are otherwise separated (see Fig. 6, right). This leads to ambiguous structures that were apparently created in the following fashion:

- Architectural rule A requires feature X
- Architectural rule B requires feature Y
- Problem: X and Y are in the same place
- Solution: Make X resemble Y in creative ways

5   Assessment

We must compare our proposed approach (Sec. 4) with the plan and requirements outlined in Sections 1 and 2. While Sec. 1 called for a shape vocabulary (Assumption 4), Sec. 2 added as further requirement its suitability for Humanities researchers to interpret shape, and proposed a digital equivalent of classical drawings (Fig. 1).

Fig. 1 is seemingly very different from Fig. 5; but we argue that their long-time sustainability is nevertheless comparable! We believe the step-by-step code in Fig. 5 is suitable as a means of communication for describing the structural decomposition of a window shape. Our prototype needs improvements like a more consistent naming of the operations, but the code, and thus, the shape structure is understandable even without an actual software implementation. Just like drawings, the code helps making explicit the implicit knowledge about shape; but the code can also be executed by a computer; parameters can be varied, and it can even be generated by a computer.

5.1   A Note on Archival, and on Metadata and Semantics

A formal shape description like in Fig. 5 is only one part of a shape information infrastructure. The available operations and their parameters must be documented, but there is no metadata standard yet for that. To achieve long-time sustainability beyond a particular software implementation, it is necessary do describe the effect of each shape operation in a complete and unambiguous way, to such a degree that it allows re-implementation on future computers. Such a documentation also clarifies the semantics of the shape description, and closes the "semantic gap" between code and its meaning. Note that once a formal description is available, it can be automatically transformed also to other encodings, such as, e.g., XML or Python, and other representations can be derived such as 2D drawings, 3D models, and renderings.

We are still a long way away, though, from a "CIDOC-CRM for 3D shape".

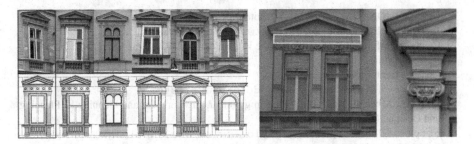

Fig. 6. Varying existing windows is substantially faster than construction from scratch. Right: Difficulties arise from overlapping structures (legde and pilaster).

6   Conclusion

In this paper we have attempted to direct the focus of attention to the problem of developing a library of domain-specific operations, rather than discussing the pros and cons of a particular procedural technology. In principle, procedural modeling is the perfect method to capture the richness and complexity of the shapes that Digital Humanities, in particular art history, have to deal with; the reason is that much of the complexity lies only in the variations. Procedural modeling is a method to "factor out" the variations and to focus more on the structure of the shapes; and this is exactly what art historians are doing all the time. The main challenge is to facilitate the process of turning implicit knowledge about shape into an explicit formal description that is amenable to digital processing. We hope we have started this process.

However, this is in fact only the point of departure of a longer journey: Art historians and historical architects have confirmed that we have in fact treated only the easy cases – art historians are used to considering much more challenging and exceptional icons of art history, and rarely treat vernacular housing as we did.

We would like to point out, however, that a formal representation can make exactly this interesting work more targeted and more pointed. As a result of our exercise we are able to produce a list of all shape phenomena to which our – admittedly very limited – set of architectural rules offers no answer; and these may be just the situations that art historians are actually interested in.

References

1. EPOCH project website, EU FP6 NoE 2004-2008, http://www.epoch-net.org
2. 3D-COFORM project website, EU FP7 IP 2008-2012, http://3dcoform.eu/
3. Tzompanaki, K., Doerr, M., Theodoridou, M., Havemann, S.: 3D-COFORM: A Large-Scale Digital Production Environment. ERCIM News 86 (July 2011)
4. Pitzalis, D., Kaminski, J., Niccolucci, F.: 3D-COFORM: Making 3D documentation an everyday choice for the cultural heritage sector. Virtual Archaeology Review 2(4), 145–146 (2011)

5. Crofts, N., Doerr, M., Stiff, M.: Definition of the CIDOC Conceptual Reference Model, ISO, iSO/PRF 21127 (2005), http://www.cidoc-crm.org/
6. Center for Information Modelling in the Humanities (ZIMiG), Graz University, http://gams.uni-graz.at/
7. Cologne Center for eHumanities, http://www.cceh.uni-koeln.de/projektliste
8. Stiny, G., Mitchell, W.J.: The Palladian grammar. Environment and Planning B: Planning and Design 5(1), 5–18 (1978), http://ideas.repec.org/a/pio/envirb/v5y1978i1p5-18.html, doi:10.1068/b050005
9. Koning, H., Eizenberg, J.: The language of the prairie: Frank Lloyd Wright's prairie houses. Environment and Planning B: Planning and Design 8(3), 295–323 (1981), http://EconPapers.repec.org/RePEc:pio:envirb:v:8:y:1981:i:3:p:295-323, doi:10.1068/b080295
10. Downing, F., Flemming, U.: The bungalows of Buffalo. Environment and Planning B: Planning and Design 8(3), 269–293 (1981), http://EconPapers.repec.org/RePEc:pio:envirb:v:8:y:1981:i:3:p:269-293, doi:10.1068/b080269
11. Flemming, U.: More than the sum of parts: the grammar of Queen Anne houses. Environment and Planning B: Planning and Design 14(3), 323–350 (1987), http://ideas.repec.org/a/pio/envirb/v14y1987i3p323-350.html, doi:10.1068/b140323
12. Buelinckx, H.: Wren's language of city church designs: a formal generative classification. Environment and Planning B: Planning and Design 20(6), 645–676 (1993), http://EconPapers.repec.org/RePEc:pio:envirb:v:20:y:1993:i:6:p:645-676, doi:10.1068/b200645
13. Duarte, J.P.: Customizing mass housing: a discursive grammar for Siza's Malagueira houses. PhD thesis, Massachusetts Institute of Technology. Dept. of Architecture (2002), http://hdl.handle.net/1721.1/8189
14. Duarte, J.P.: Towards the mass customization of housing: the grammar of Siza's houses at Malagueira. Environment and Planning B: Planning and Design 32(3), 347–380 (2005), http://EconPapers.repec.org/RePEc:pio:envirb:v:32:y:2005:i:3:p:347-380, doi:10.1068/b31124
15. Duarte, J.P., Rocha, J.A.M., Soares, G.D.: Unveiling the structure of the Marrakech Medina: A shape grammar and an interpreter for generating urban form. Artif. Intell. Eng. Des. Anal. Manuf. 21(4), 317–349 (2007), http://dx.doi.org/10.1017/S0890060407000315, doi:10.1017/S0890060407000315
16. Müller, P., Vereenhoghe, T., Wonka, P., Paap, I., Van Gool, L.: Procedural 3D Reconstruction of Puuc buildings in Xkipche. In: Proc. VAST 2006, pp. 139–146. Eurographics Association, Aire-la-Ville (2006)
17. Dylla, K., Müller, P., Ulmer, A., Haegler, S., Frischer, B.: Rome Reborn 2.0: A Case Study of Virtual City Reconstruction Using Procedural Modeling Techniques. In: Proc. CAA 2009, Williamsburg, Virginia, pp. 62–66. Archaeopress, Oxford (2010)
18. Fassi, F., Parri, S.: Complex Architecture in 3D: From Survey to Web. International Journal of Heritage in the Digital Era (IJHDE) 1(3), 379–398 (2012), http://dx.doi.org/10.1260/2047-4970.1.3.379,   doi:10.1260/2047-4970.1.3.379

19. De Luca, L., Veron, P., Florenzano, M.: A generic formalism for the semantic modeling and representation of architectural elements. The Visual Computer 23(3), 181–205 (2007), doi:10.1007/s00371-006-0092-5
20. Havemann, S.: Generative Mesh Modeling. PhD thesis, Braunschweig University of Technology (2005)
21. Havemann, S., Fellner, D.W.: Generative parametric design of gothic window tracery. In: Proc. VAST 2004, pp. 193–201 (2004), doi:10.2312/VAST/VAST04/193-201
22. Gerth, B., Berndt, R., Havemann, S., Fellner, D.W.: 3D modeling for nonexpert users with the Castle Construction Kit v0.5. In: Proc. VAST 2005 Intl. Symp., pp. 49–57. Eurographics (2005), doi:10.2312/VAST/VAST05/049-057
23. Hohmann, B., Havemann, S., Krispel, U., Fellner, D.W.: A GML shape grammar for semantically enriched 3D building models. Computers & Graphics 34(4), 322–334 (2010), http://dx.doi.org/10.1016/j.cag.2010.05.007
24. Zmugg, R., Krispel, U., Thaller, W., Havemann, S., Pszeida, M., Fellner, D.W.: A new approach for interactive procedural modelling in cultural heritage. In: Proceedings of the 40th Conference of Computer Applications and Quantitative Methods in Archaeology (CAA 2012) (2012)
25. Havemann, S., Fellner, D.W.: Towards a New Shape Description Paradigm Using the Generative Modeling Language. In: Calude, C.S., Rozenberg, G., Salomaa, A. (eds.) Rainbow of Computer Science. LNCS, vol. 6570, pp. 200–214. Springer, Heidelberg (2011)
26. Thaller, W., Zmugg, R., Krispel, U., Posch, M., Havemann, S., Pszeida, M., Fellner, D.W.: Creating procedural window building blocks using the generative fact labeling method. In: Boehm, J., Kersten, T., Fuse, T., Remondino, F. (eds.) Proceedings of the 5th ISPRS International Workshop 3D-ARCH 2013, ISPRS (2013)

Geometric Issues in Reconstruction of Virtual Heritage Involving Large Populations

Daniel Thalmann[1], Barbara Maïm[2], and Jonathan Maïm[2]

[1] Institute for Media Innovation, Nanyang Technological University and EPFL, Switzerland
danielthalmann@ntu.edu.sg, daniel.thalmann@epfl.ch
[2] Minsh, Lausanne, Switzerland
Barbara@minsh.net, Jonathan.Maim@gmail.com

Abstract. This Chapter discusses the methods involved in the generation of large crowds of Virtual Humans in environments like cities. We focus on the geometric aspects of these methods in the different steps involved: scaler, simulator, renderer, path planner, and behaviour handler. We emphasize the application of these methods to the field of Cultural Heritage, recreating old cities with population living their life. In particular, we present examples from Pompeii and discuss the interaction between the environment and the behaviour of the Romans.

Keywords: Crowd Simulation, Behavioral Animation, LODs, Path Planning, Region Of Interest, Scaler, Behavior Handler, Simulation of crowd collisions.

1   Introduction

In this chapter, we survey the methods that allow the generation of large crowds of people to represent inhabited cities of the past. Our objective is to create and animate Interactive Virtual Crowds made of thousands of walking pedestrians, in order to massively populate given environments. To reach this objective, we need first to create various individuals from a small set of templates. A template defines the general appearance of a human - male or female, adult or child, etc – which is declined to compute the exact appearance of a given individual: variations in shape, height, texture, clothes, hair, skin color, motion style, accessories are introduced (see [1] for more details). A human template, consists of

- A skeleton, composed of joints, representing articulations,
- A set of meshes, all representing the same virtual human, but with a decreasing number of triangles,
- Several appearance sets, used to vary its appearance,
- A set of animation sequences which it can play.

Each rendered virtual human is derived from a human template, i.e., it is an instance of a human template. In order for all the instances of a same human template to look different, we use several appearance sets, that allow to vary the texture applied to the instances, and modulate the colors of the texture.

M. Ioannides and E. Quak (Eds.): 3D Research Challenges, LNCS 8355, pp. 78–92, 2014.
© Springer-Verlag Berlin Heidelberg 2014

The second component allows simulating pedestrians' navigation. The environment geometry is preprocessed in order to distinguish navigable parts from obstacles. With certain directives, users can attribute navigation goals to batches of pedestrians in order to handle large crowds easily; however, the process results in unique individual trajectories in order to preserve variety in motion. Finally, the third component is the real-time pipeline, dedicated to the run-time computations.

These computations first include the steering of virtual humans, by the simulator, along paths computed at the preliminary navigation planning stage. Second, the animator component computes the posture of each human according to the steering. Finally, humans are rendered to the screen in a final step, with respect to their individual visual appearance. At all steps of the real-time pipeline [2], we exploit a level-of-detail approach in order to enhance animation and rendering quality for humans at the forefront, according to the spectator's point of view. Section 2 will describe the steps involved in this real-time pipeline in details.

The structure we use is based on a dedicated cell-decomposition technique called navigation graph [3 4]: from a 3D model of a scene, a navigation graph is automatically derived. It captures and models both the geometry and the topology of the navigable space. The navigation graph is used as a basic structure to categorize the environment into regions of various interests. With the same concept of levels of detail we use for rendering, regions of high/medium/low interest are identified in the environment, and ruled by different motion planning algorithms. Each algorithm, in its own way, provides waypoints to steer virtual humans in real-time. A second interesting aspect of navigation graphs is to use them for triggering situation-based behaviors. Using a semantic model of the environment (see Figure 1), the navigation graph is augmented with semantic data to develop crowd behaviors: specific actions are triggered in desired areas of the environment.

Fig. 1. Some examples of Navigation Graphs automatically computed from the geometry of virtual environments

2 Related Work

Virtual crowds are composed of a large number of Virtual Humans [5]. A Virtual Human is classically defined as a computer-generated character with the appearance of a human being. Two types of Virtual Humans are very common: Avatars [6] and Virtual Agents. An Avatar is the graphical representation of the user or the user's alter ego or character. It may take either a three-dimensional form, as in games or virtual worlds, or a two-dimensional form as an icon in Internet forums and other online communities. Avatars became very popular with Second Life [7]. Virtual Agents are interactive characters that exhibit human-like qualities and communicate with humans or with each other using natural human modalities such as speech and gesture. Virtual agents are capable of real-time perception, cognition and action that allow them to participate in a dynamic social environment. Virtual agents don't need to have a human appearance. Finally, many people use the term Autonomous Virtual Humans, which roughly corresponds to Virtual Agents with a Human appearance. In the remainder of this Chapter, we will use the term Virtual Humans as equivalent to autonomous Virtual Humans.

The first studied approach, i.e., agent-based, represents a natural way to simulate crowds as independent individuals interacting with each other. Such algorithms usually handle short distance avoidance, and navigation remains local. Reynolds [8] proposed to use simple rules to model crowds of interacting agents. Heïgeas et al. [9] introduced a physically-based interactive particle system to model emergent crowd behavior often encountered in emergency situation. Kirchner and Shadschneider [10] used static potential fields to rule a cellular automaton. Metoyer and Hodgins [11] proposed an avoidance algorithm based on a Bayesian decision process.

To solve the problems inherent in local navigation, some behavioral approaches have been extended with global navigation. Bayazit et al. [12] stored global information in nodes of a probabilistic roadmap to handle navigation. Sung et al. [13], given constraints at specific time intervals on character poses, positions, and orientations, used a motion graph to generate the adequate motion. Lau and Kuffner [14] used precomputed search trees of motion clips to accelerate the search for the best paths and motion sequences to reach an objective. Lamarche and Donikian [15] used automatic topological model extraction of the environment for navigation. Another method, introduced by Kamphuis and Overmars [16], allows a group of agents to stay together while trying to reach a goal. Although these approaches offer appealing results, they are not fast enough to simulate thousands of pedestrians in real time. Loscos et al. [17] proposed to steer pedestrians in a city with probabilistic rules, and based on a 2D map of the city building imprints. Their method is suited for simulating wandering crowds, but does not provide high level control on pedestrian goals. Pettré et al. presented the navigation graph, a structure automatically extracted from an environment geometry, allowing to solve global path planning requests [3 4]. The main advantage of this technique is that it handles uneven and multilayered terrains. Nevertheless, it does not treat inter-pedestrian collision avoidance. Finally, Helbing et al. [18 19] used agent-based approaches to handle motion planning, but mainly focused on emergent crowd behaviors in particular scenarios.

Another approach for motion planning is inspired from fluid dynamics. Such techniques use a grid to discretize the environment into cells. Hughes [20] used density fields to steer pedestrians toward their goal and avoid collisions. Chenney [21] used flow tiles to represent small stationary regions of velocity fields that can be pieced together to drive crowds. More recently, Treuille et al. [22] used a dynamic potential field to represent the best path to a goal. Pedestrians are steered according to the potential gradient, avoiding collision with the environment and other pedestrians. Fluid dynamics represent an interesting solution in applications where the lack of individuality of each pedestrian is unimportant. Indeed, these solutions are usually meant to steer large groups of avatars towards a shared goal. Recently, a new branch of research tries to extract patterns from real pedestrian avoidance behaviors in order to rule their models, [23 24 25]. As of today, the obtained performance does not fit to large interactive crowds. More detail about crowd simulation could be found in [26].

3   The Six Major Real-Time Stages

For this representation of scenes with large crowds, we have six major real-time stages: Scaler, Simulator, Animator, Renderer, Path Planner, and Behavior Handler. For each stage, there are important geometric issues to consider in order to be able to simulate crowds in real-time. Efficient crowd simulation is obtained by targeting computing resources where the attention of the user is focused.

1. The **Scaler** is the first stage of the pipeline. The work done in this stage consists in finding which simulation and rendering level-of-detail is used for which area of the scene for the current simulation frame.
2. The **Simulator** ensures that each virtual human instance comes closer to its next waypoint, i.e., its next short-term goal.
3. The **Animator** is responsible for the animation of each virtual human, whichever the representation it is using, i.e., deformable mesh, rigid mesh, or impostor. It modifies the human's posture to reflect the locomotion or idle change according to the steering.
4. The **Renderer** represents the phase where draw calls are carefully issued to the GPU to display the environment and the crowd. It displays efficiently the varied human instances, with their projected shadows, and the environment.
5. The **Path Planner** is responsible for avoiding inter-pedestrian collisions.
6. The **Behavior Handler** takes care of updating the crowd behavior, according to some high-level rules.

4   The Scaler

The Scaler is the first stage of the pipeline. The work done in this stage consists in finding which simulation and rendering level-of-detail (see Figure 2) is used for which area of the scene for the current simulation frame. User focus is determined by simple rules that allow to spread computing resources throughout the environment. The Scaler receives two inputs: a navigation graph filled with virtual human identifiers and a camera view frustum. From these inputs, the Scaler's role is to provide each navigation graph vertex with two scores. Firstly, a level of detail (LOD), determined by finding the distance from the vertex to the camera and its eccentricity from the middle of the screen. This LOD score is then used to choose the appropriate virtual human representation inside the vertex. Secondly, the Scaler associates with each vertex a score of interest, resulting in an environment divided into regions of different interest (ROI). For each region, we choose a different motion planning algorithm. Regions of high interest use accurate, but more costly techniques, while regions of lower interest may exploit simpler methods. At the end of this first stage, we obtain two lists. The first one, the rendering list, contains all virtual human ids, sorted by human template, by LOD, and finally by appearance set. The second list, the navigation list, contains occupied vertices, sorted by ROI.

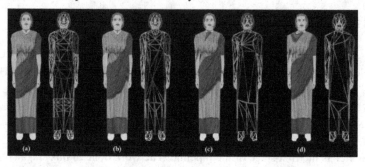

Fig. 2. Different LODs for a model, from left to right : lod0 with 1042 triangles (a), lod1 with 824 triangles (b), lod2 with 652 triangles (c), lod3   with 519 triangles (d)

Using the navigation graph as a hierarchical structure to provide virtual humans with scores is an efficient technique that allows to avoid testing individually each character. The processing of data is achieved as follows: firstly, each vertex of the graph is tested against the camera view frustum. Empty vertices are not even scored, nor further held in the process for the current frame; indeed, there is no interest to keep them in the subsequent stages of the pipeline. On the other hand, vertices filled with at least one character and outside the camera view are kept, but they are not assigned any LOD score, since they are outside the view frustum, and thus, their virtual humans are not displayed. As for their ROI score, they get the lowest one: a minimal simulation sporadically moves the related virtual humans along their path, and no dynamic collision avoidance need be achieved. This minimal simulation is necessary, even though the characters are invisible, because without care, when they quit the camera field, they immediately stop moving, and thus, get packed on the borders of the view frustum, causing a disturbing effect for the user. Finally, the vertices that are filled and visible are assigned a higher ROI score, and then are further investigated to sort their embedded virtual humans by human template, LOD, and appearance set.

5   The Simulator

The purpose of the second stage of the pipeline, the simulator, is to ensure that each pedestrian comes closer to its next waypoint. Indeed, each virtual human stores a waypoint, which is the position of its next short-term goal to reach. Note that the manner in which this update and the next waypoints are computed directly depends on the ROI in which the pedestrians are situated. Depending on the ROI, path smoothing is applied, and efficient internal book-keeping of the Virtual Humans on the underlying navigation graph is done. More details can be found in [27].

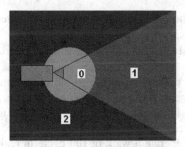

Fig. 3. The three Regions Of Interest

We consider 3 Regions of Interest, dependent on the camera, as shown in Figure 3:

- Level 0: regions of high interest are typically zones in front of the camera, or where particular events are happening. Such regions are governed by a potential field-based algorithm similar to [19], based on a precomputed grid. Note that in regions of this level of interest, pedestrians are steered towards special waypoints corresponding to the center of a neighbor cell with the lowest potential. The navigation graph waypoints are not used here.
- Level 1: in regions still visible but of lower interest, pedestrians are smoothly steered towards their navigation graph waypoint. In addition, a short-term collision avoidance method is exploited: taking advantage of the grid structure, a pedestrian checks in the cells ahead if another pedestrian is close by. If it is the case, an intermediate waypoint is introduced to avoid the collision. Once the collision is resolved, the pedestrian is assigned its next navigation graph waypoint again, and resumes its progress on its path.
- Level 2: in regions of no interest, i.e., outside the camera view frustum, pedestrians are steered linearly towards their next navigation graph waypoint and do not perform any collision avoidance.

6   The Animator

The Animator, the third stage of the real-time pipeline, is responsible for the animation of each virtual human, whichever the representation it is using, i.e., deformable mesh, rigid mesh, or impostor. The lists of visible virtual humans, sorted by human template, LOD, and appearance set in the Scaler phase, are the main data structure used in this stage.

The third stage is responsible for animating characters whichever the representation they are using. We use three different representations decreasingly costly to render and animate :

- dynamic meshes, which are deformed in real time using a skeleton and a skinning technique,
- static meshes, whose deformations are pre-computed for a chosen selection of animation clips,
- impostors, extensively exploited in the domain of crowd rendering.

The runtime animation process is similar for all representations: depending on the pedestrian's current animation time, the correct keyframe is identified and retrieved. Then, each representation is modified accordingly. We use the locomotion engine of Glardon et al. [28] to generate various locomotion cycles (see Figure 4). Although this engine is fast enough to generate a walk or run cycle in real-time, it cannot keep up that rhythm with thousands of virtual humans. The idea of precomputing a series of locomotion cycles and storing them in a database came up then.

Fig. 4. Walking crowd

7   The Renderer

The Renderer represents the phase where draw calls are carefully issued to the GPU to display the environment and the crowd. Indeed, it is important to minimize first the state changes overhead, and second, the number of draw calls. In our architecture, illumination ambiances are set from four directional lights, whose direction and diffuse and ambient colors are beforehand (or interactively) defined by the designer. The light coming from the sun is the only one casting shadows. As we lack a real-time global illumination system, the three other lights are present to provide enough freedom for the designer to give a realistic look to the scene. This configuration has given us satisfaction as we mainly work on outdoor scenes. An example is shown in Figure 5.

Fig. 5. A rendered crowd

Virtual humans cast shadows on the environment and, reciprocally, the environment casts shadows on them. This is achieved using a shadow mapping algorithm [29] implemented on the GPU. Once the first pass has been executed, the second pass is used to render all the virtual humans and their shadows. To reduce state change overhead, the number of draw calls is minimized, thanks to our rendering list of visible humans sorted by human template, LOD and appearance set.

In this rendering phase, one can see the full power of the sorted lists: all the instances of the same deformable mesh have the same vertices, normals and texture coordinates, Thus, these coordinates need to be bound only once per deformable mesh LOD. The same applies for the appearance sets: even though they are used by several virtual humans, each needs to be sent only once to the GPU. For the rigid meshes, the process is quite different, since all the vertex deformations have been achieved in a pre-process. In the rendering phase of the rigid meshes, only the texture coordinates and indices can be bound at the LOD level, in opposition to the deformable meshes, where all mesh data is bound at this level. The reason is obvious: for a deformable mesh, all the components representing its mesh information (vertices, normals, etc.) are the same for all instances. It is only later, on the GPU, that the mesh is deformed to fit the skeleton posture of each individual. Rendering impostors is fast, thanks to the animation list, which is sorted by human template, appearance set, animation, and keyframe, and is updated in the Animator phase.

8   The Path Planner

The path planner stage performs the collision avoidance between pedestrians. Due to a complexity of $O(n^2)$, it runs at a significantly lower frequency than the previous stages. Regions of high interest, typically in the vicinity of the camera, are treated with a long-term collision avoidance strategy, while other ROIs are treated with short-term algorithms.

No inter-pedestrian collision is performed in regions of no interest (ROI 2). In other regions, called of "low" interest, i.e., visible zones that are situated at far distances, and/or where no special event is happening, we need an efficient short-term avoidance algorithm. Our ideal algorithm should be very fast, for it manages a large number of pedestrians, and usable in both ROI 1 and ROI 0 (in cases of very narrow or crowded places (e.g. Figure 6), where the potential field approach may fail).

Fig. 6. A crowded place

We have designed a short-term avoidance algorithm based on the assumptions that pedestrians mostly want to first maximize their speed and second, to minimize detours.

Algorithm 1. Short-term avoidance algorithm

Data: set of pedestrians in $\{ROI\ 0 \cup ROI\ 1\}$, set of grid cells, distances α and β
Result: new set of pedestrians in $\{ROI\ 0 \cup ROI\ 1\}$

1 **if** $isEven(frameNumber)$ **then**
2   **for** $each\ pedestrian\ p \in \{ROI\ 0 \cup ROI\ 1\}$ **do**
3   register p in its current cell c_p

4 **else**
5   **for** $each\ pedestrian\ p\ in\ cell\ c_p$ **do**
6          $Set_{neighbors} = findNeighbors(c_p, \alpha)$
7   **for** $each\ pedestrian\ p_{neighbor}\ in\ Set_{neighbors}$ **do**
8   **if** $distance(p, p_{neighbor}) < \beta$ **then**
9   slide p away from $p_{neighbor}$
10   **else if** $angle(p, p_{neighbor}) \in [-\frac{\pi}{4}, \frac{\pi}{4}]$ **then**
11                  $rotateWaypoint(p, p_{neighbor})$

Another aspect of crowds we addressed is the simulation of small groups of people. Indeed, in real life, it is rare to observe people walking alone, and flocking behaviors are necessary to obtain realistic results.

9   The Behavior Handler

Finally, the last stage of the crowd pipeline is the behavior handler. During the entire pipeline, virtual humans cannot change their current animation type, e.g., from loco-motion to idle, because it would invalidate the various sorted lists of the system. This last stage is thus the only one which is allowed to change the motivation and current animation type of virtual humans. It is always achieved at the end of the pipeline, for the next frame. Crowd behavior is situation-based, i.e., behavior is updated indivi-dually for each virtual human, based on their position in the Navigation Graph. An optional semantic model can be used as a second input to generate a navigation graph annotated with high-level information. Such a model is usually a simplified environ-ment geometry demarcating zones where specific behaviors are expected from pede-strians. For instance, a semantic model could provide positions of show windows, so that pedestrians look at these points when passing nearby, or areas where shops are situated so that individuals are provided with shopping bags before leaving the shop. Technically, such areas are identified in the semantic model, and all graph vertices enclosed within this area are tagged with a specific behavior. When a pedestrian enters this zone, it will perform the associated action.

10   Case Study: Populating Ancient Pompeii with Crowds

Pompeii was a Roman city, destroyed and completely buried during a catastrophic eruption of the volcano Mount Vesuvius. We have revived its glorious past using a 3D model of its former appearance and populated it with crowds[30] (see Fig. 7). In an offline process, the city is first automatically reconstructed and exported into two different representations:

- A high-resolution model. It is used to generate a Navigation Graph, and is also rendered at runtime.
- A low-resolution model labeled with semantic data. This model is only composed of annotated building footprints and door / window positions.

From this annotated geometry, we automatically label the Navigation Graph ver-tices with the correct actions to be performed by the Virtual Romans. In Table 1, we summarize the different semantics that have been embedded in the city geometry and the associated behaviors we want to trigger in the crowd. We only list a small set of behaviors. Many more behaviors could easily be added.

Fig. 7. Crowds of Virtual Romans in a street of Ancient Pompeii

Table 1. Summary of semantics and associated behaviors

geometry semantics	behavior	actions
shop	get amphora	walk inside, get out with am-
bakery	get bread	walk inside, get out with bread.
young	rich	only rich people go there.
old	poor	only poor people go there.
door	look at	slow down, look through it.
window	look at	slow down, look through it.
	stop look at	accelerate, stop looking.

There are several buildings in the city model where virtual Romans can freely enter. Some of them are labelled as shops and bakeries, and the characters entering them acquire related accessories, e.g., oil amphoras or bread. These accessories are directly attached to a joint of the virtual character's skeleton, and follow its movements when deformed. We can attach accessories to various joints, depending on their nature. Here, we illustrate this variety by empirically placing the amphoras in the hands or on the heads of the Romans, depending on their social rank. The idea of rich and poor districts is based on age maps that were provided by archaeologists taking part in this project. These maps show the age of buildings in the city. Using them, it is possible to see where the districts that have been most recently built are situated. Although this age difference cannot yet be expressed with various textures on the buildings, we have empirically decided to set the rich Roman templates in the most recent districts and the poor people in older areas. From this, virtual characters know where they belong and while most parts of the city are accessible to everybody, some districts are restricted to a certain class of people: rich Romans in most recent districts and slaves in the oldest zones. When the virtual Romans walk in the city, they may pass near an open door or a window. In this case, we make the characters slow down and look at them.

Fig. 8. (left) A middle-class Virtual Roman carries amphoras in its hands and also on its head, while (right) a rich Virtual Roman may carry bread in its hands, but would not bear anything on its head

We know that each semantic label corresponds to a specific behavior. For instance, the window and door semantics trigger a "look at" behavior that makes Virtual Romans slow down and look through the window (see Table 1). To keep our crowd engine as generic as possible, each graph vertex triggering a special behavior also receives a series of variables used later on for parameterization. For our "look at" example, this means that each graph vertex associated with this behavior should make Romans look through the window or the door. In order to know exactly where Romans have to look, each of these graph vertices also receives a target point, computed as the center of the window/door quad.

There are many behaviors that can be triggered when a Virtual Roman passes over a graph vertex. Some of them are permanent, i.e., once they are triggered for a Roman, they are kept until the end of the simulation, while others are temporary: once the Roman leaves their area, the behaviors are stopped. For instance, a Roman entering a bakery acquires some bread and will keep it when leaving the bakery until the end of the simulation. However, a Roman passing close to a window will slow down to look through it until it is too far away and then resume a faster walk. The permanent behaviors are not complex to manage. Once triggered, they modify parameters within the Roman data that will never be set back to their previous value. For temporary behaviors however, it is important to detect when a Roman leaves an area with a specific behavior, and set his modified parameters back to normal values.

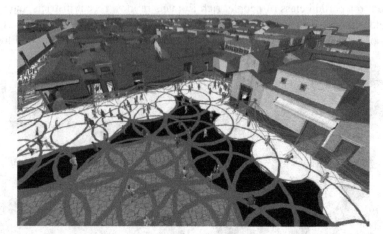

Fig. 9. Graph vertices are marked with special behaviors: "look at" (in white), and "stop look at" (in black). The target points where the Romans should look are indicated in red.

For the crowds, combining the different LOD, it is possible to simulate in this environment 4,000 Romans, i.e., about 600,000 triangles and 88 Mb of compressed textures, with real-time performance (30 fps in average).

11   Conclusion

In this Chapter, we have explained how we can represent cities with large crowds, and particularly cities of ancient times. We have emphasized the geometric issues for the six major real-time stages: Scaler, Simulator, Animator, Renderer, Path Planner, and Behavior Handler. We have focused on the behavior handler in our case study on populating the ancient city of Pompeii.

References

1. Yersin, B., Maïm, J., Thalmann, D.: Unique Instances for Crowds. IEEE Computer Graphics and Applications 29(6), 82–90 (2009)
2. Maïm, J., Yersin, B., Pettré, J., Thalmann, D.: YaQ: An Architecture for Real-Time Navigation and Rendering of Varied Crowds. IEEE Computer Graphics and Applications 29(4), 44–53 (2009)
3. Pettré, J., de HerasCiechomski, P., Maïm, J., Yersin, B., Laumond, J.P., Thalmann, D.: Real-time navigating crowds: scalable simulation and rendering: Research articles. Comput. Animat. Virtual Worlds 17(3-4), 445–455 (2006)
4. Pettré, J., Grillon, H., Thalmann, D.: Crowds of moving objects: Navigation plan-ning and simulation. In: Proceedings of IEEE International Conference on Robotics and Automation, pp. 3062–3067 (2007)
5. Magnenat-Thalmann, N., Thalmann, D.: Handbook of Virtual Humans. John Wiley (2004)

6. Çapin, T., Pandzic, I., Magnenat Thalmann, N., Thalmann, D.: Avatars in Networked Virtual Environments. John Wiley (1999)
7. http://secondlife.com/
8. Reynolds, C.W.: Flocks, herds and schools: A distributed behavioral model. In: SIGGRAPH 1987: Proceedings of the 14th Annual Conference on Computer Graphics and Interactive Techniques, pp. 25–34. ACM Press, New York (1987)
9. Heigeas, L., Luciani, A., Thollot, J., Castagné, N.: A physically-basedparticle model of emergent crowd behaviors. In: Graphicon (2003)
10. Kirchner, A., Shadschneider, A.: Simulation of evacuation processes using abionics-inspired cellular automaton model for pedestrian dynamics. Physica A, 237–244 (2001)
11. Ronald, A., Metoyer, R.A., Hodgins, J.K.: Reactive pedestrian path following from examples. In: CASA 20: Proceedings of the 16th International Conference on ComputerAnimation and Social Agents (CASA 2003), p. 149. IEEEComputer Society, Washington, DC (2003)
12. Bayazit, O.B., Lien, J.M., Amato, N.M.: Better group behaviors in complexenvironments using global roadmaps. In: Proceedings of the Eighth International Conference on Artificial Life, pp. 362–370. MITPress, Cambridge (2003)
13. Sung, M., Kovar, L., Gleicher, M.: Fast and accurate goal-directed motionsynthesis for crowds. In: SCA 2005: Proceedings of the 2005 ACM SIGGRAPH/Eurographics Symposium on Computer Animation, pp. 291–300. ACM Press, New York (2005)
14. Lau, M., Kuffner, J.: Precomputed search trees: Planning for interactive goaldrive-nanimation. In: ACM SIGGRAPH / Eurographics Symposium on Computer Animation, pp. 299–308 (September 2006)
15. Lamarche, F., Donikian, S.: Crowd of virtual humans: a new approach forreal time navigation in complex and structured environments. Computer Graphics Forum 23(3), 509–518 (2004)
16. Kamphuis, A., Overmars, M.H.: Finding paths for coherent groups using clear-ance. In: SCA 2004: Proceedings of the 2004 ACM SIGGRAPH/Eurographics Symposium on Computer Animation, pp. 19–28 (2004)
17. Loscos, C., Marchal, D., Meyer, A.: Intuitive crowd behaviour in denseurban environments using local laws. In: TPCG 2003: Proceedings of the Theory and Practice of Computer Graphics, Washington, DC, USA, p. 122 (2003)
18. Helbing, D., Molnár, P., Schweitzer, F.: Computer simulations of pedestrian dynamics and trail formation. Evolution of Natural Structures, 229–234 (1994)
19. Helbing, D., Farkas, I., Vicsek, T.: Simulating dynamical features of escape panic. Nature 407(6803), 487–490 (2000)
20. Hughes, R.L.: A continuum theory for the flow of pedestrians. Transportation Research PartB: Methodological 36(29), 507–535 (2002)
21. Chenney, S.: Flow tiles. In: SCA 2004: Proceedings of the 2004 ACM SIGGRAPH/Eurographics Symposium on Computer Animation, Aire-la-Ville, Switzerland, pp. 233–242 (2004)
22. Treuille, A., Cooper, S., Popović, Z.: Continuum crowds. In: SIGGRAPH 2006:ACM SIGGRAPH 2006 Papers, pp. 1160–1168. ACM, New York (2006)
23. Lerner, A., Chrysanthou, Y., Lischinski, D.: Crowds by example. Eurographics 2007: ComputerGraphics Forum 26(3) (2007)
24. Paris, S., Pettré, J., Donikian, S.: Pedestrian reactive for crowd simulation: A predictive approach. Computer Graphics Forum 26(3), 665–674 (2007), Eurographics 2007

25. Hoon Lee, K., Geol Choi, M., Hong, Q., Lee, J.: Group behavior from video: a datadrive-napproach to crowd simulation. In: SCA 2007: Proceedings of the 2007 ACM SIGGRAPH/Eurographics Symposium on Computer Animation, pp. 109–118 (2007)
26. Thalmann, D., Musse, S.R.: Crowd Simulation, 2nd edn. Springer (2012)
27. Morini, F., Yersin, B., Maïm, J., Thalmann, D.: Real-Time Scalable Motion Planning for Crowds. The Visual Computer 24(10), 859–870 (2008)
28. Glardon, P., Boulic, R., Thalmann, D.: PCA-based walking engine using motioncap-ture data. In: Proc. of Computer Graphics International, pp. 292–298 (2004)
29. Williams, L.: Casting curved shadows on curved surfaces. In: SIGGRAPH 1978: Procee-dingsof the 5th Annual Conference on Computer Graphics and Interactive Techniques, pp. 270–274. ACM Press, NY (1978)
30. Maïm, J., Haegler, S., Yersin, B., Müller, P., Thalmann, D., Van Gool, L.: Populating Ancient Pompeii with Crowds of Virtual Romans. In: The 8th International Symposium on Virtual Reality, Archaeology and Cultural Heritage (VAST 2007), pp. 109–116 (2007)

Going to the Movies:
Lessons from the Film Industry for 3D Libraries

Neil A. Dodgson

The Computer Laboratory, University of Cambridge,
15 J J Thomson Avenue, Cambridge, UK CB3 0FD
Neil.Dodgson@cl.cam.ac.uk

Abstract. The film industry can provide insights for researchers in cultural heritage. Modern movies require the management of an enormous number of digital assets, analogous to how digital assets are managed in cultural heritage. Furthermore, movies are cultural artefacts in their own right: the preservation of movies gives lessons in the preservation of other ephemera, including all of those digital assets. Finally, some movies use historical contexts and there are lessons in why collaboration between cultural historians and movie-makers can be unsatisfying.

Keywords: Culture, heritage, history, film, movie, 3D, modelling.

1 Introduction

Cultural heritage applications often involve the acquisition or creation of 3D models. Two industries drive development in 3D modelling: games and movies. The use of 3D modelling in movie production is either ahead of academic research or actively using the most recent academic research. Key milestones in the history of 3D modelling in the movies are:

Jurassic Park (1993), widely regarded as the first major motion picture to use photorealistic digitally created 3D characters in a central role.

Toy Story (1995), the first feature film with completely computer-rendered 3D characters.

Final Fantasy (2001), the first computer-generated animated motion picture with photo-realistic 3D humanoid characters.

Avatar (2009), large-scale use of live-action motion capture that directly drove computer-generated 3D rendering.

The rise in use of 3D models has been dramatic. It is now possible to make a live-action movie that is largely rendered from 3D models and almost all major animated motion pictures are now rendered in fully-realised 3D worlds. The largest visual effects companies (e.g., Pixar, Disney, Weta) today have their own research divisions, which publish in the major research venues. This multi-million euro industry has the resources to create 3D models of stunning quality. It has to manage large volumes of data. In many ways, it provides lessons for the use of 3D modelling in cultural heritage.

M. Ioannides and E. Quak (Eds.): 3D Research Challenges, LNCS 8355, pp. 93–103, 2014.
© Springer-Verlag Berlin Heidelberg 2014

With regard to managing digital 3D libraries, the American Academy of Motion Pictures Art and Sciences reports: "Current practices in other sectors such as medical, earth science, government, corporate businesses and supercomputing have spotlighted two major findings of interest to the motion picture industry: (1) Every enterprise has similar problems and issues with digital data preservation. (2) No enterprise yet has a long-term strategy or solution that does not require significant and on-going capital investment and operational expense." [1]

Most of this paper is concerned with lessons that can be learnt from the film industry. However, I begin by considering movies as cultural heritage in their own right. In particular, asking how well we have been preserving movies for posterity.

2   Movies as Cultural Artefacts

I visited CineSite in London in 2008 [2]. My host expressed concern about how many movies remained undigitised in the British Film Institute (BFI) archive. This is a big problem: the BFI has an archive of 150,000 movies: a thousand million feet (300,000 kilometers) of physical film. These movies are themselves only one third of the BFI's total archive of footage [3]. I was given the impression that time was pressing and that the BFI risked losing precious heritage to the inevitable deterioration of physical media. However, further investigation reveals that this is overly pessimistic. Stored correctly, physical film has a better chance of survival than some digital media.

2.1   Preserving Film

Physical film has interesting properties that make it challenging to store. It is constructed from layers of different materials on a robust but flexible substrate. It can fail in several ways. For example, the layers can detach from one another making replay impossible and reconstruction difficult [4]. More dramatic are some of the failure modes of the flexible substrate. The earliest films used nitrocellulose. It was chosen because it has the required flexibility and robustness. Unfortunately it is also highly flammable. This *nitrate* film has a tendency to burst into flame spontaneously, and then to burn uncontrollably because its combustion releases oxygen that fuels further combustion. Despite this challenging drawback, it was used in the early decades of movie production because there was no other cheap material with the required properties.

Acetate film replaced nitrate film in the early 1950s. Acetate film does not spontaneously combust. Unfortunately, after many years of using acetate, it was discovered that it has its own dramatic failure mode. If stored in poor conditions, the film slowly releases acetic acid (the acid in vinegar). This causes the film substrate to become brittle and shrink, destroying the ability to play it back and badly affecting the image quality. Worse still, acetic acid fumes from one reel of film initiate decay in any reels stored nearby, thereby multiplying the loss. Nitrate film is, of course, even more dramatic in its multiplicative loss, because the combustion of a single reel of nitrate film can lead to the loss of an entire archive to fire.

To someone indoctrinated in the superiority of digital media, this bodes ill for the future preservation of movies. Simply put: a lot of archive material is preserved only on film and film deteriorates over time. However, the situation is not as bad as it seems. Organisations like the BFI invest heavily in preservation. Some film has already survived reasonably intact over 70 years [3]. More crucially, our understanding of ideal storage conditions has improved dramatically over the last century [4]. We now know the ideal conditions for preservation of acetate and nitrate film. They need to be stored cold and dry. That is, near freezing point (0°C) and at low relative humidity (below about 40%). In these conditions, we expect physical film to remain intact and usable for centuries [4].

Compare this to storage on digital media. Half-inch digital archive tape (LTO Ultrium) has a predicted life of 30 years [5]. While impressive, for digital media, it is far short of the centuries promised for physical film. Furthermore, digital media bring other issues: we must preserve the playback mechanism, spare parts for the playback mechanism, and software that can interpret the digital format. In contrast to the view that physical film is a poor storage medium, it seems that preserving movies on physical film may be a better bet than preserving them on digital tape.

However, digital tape is decreasingly used for archive. The trend is to keep archives on permanently spinning media. By using disc, and by continually upgrading and updating the disc store, we are able to guarantee storage for as long as the electricity supply continues and for as long as we can buy those upgrades and updates to the disc store. Furthermore, just as disc supplanted tape, it is possible that solid-state memory will replace disc as the storage medium of choice.

But this does not solve the whole problem. There is also the question of format and playback. Physical film is well-understood and the methods of playback have changed little in decades. By contrast, new digital formats are constantly being introduced and existing formats updated. In 2008–10, the American Academy of Motion Pictures Art and Sciences undertook a case study in digital preservation [6], considering archive of two hours of film and associated media. Although the project concerned itself with archiving only film and photographs, the team still had to deal with seven known file types and several unknown (and therefore unarchivable) file types. Another report from the same organisation [1] estimates that the annual cost of preserving archival footage is about US$1,000 per title on physical film but US$12,500 in digital formats owing to the significant and perpetual spending required to maintain accessibility of digital media.

So, the first lessons we learn from the movies are that the digital brings a slew of new problems not faced by physical storage and that preservation of any medium requires continual investment. We can preserve movies as cultural artefacts for a long time, provided we have sufficient funds either to pay for the air conditioning in our physical film stores or to pay for continual upgrades and replacements of disc drives and software in our digital stores. The good news is that, so long as we maintain a necessary level of investment (and of civilisation), we can essentially achieve permanent archive.

2.2   Lost Movies

This discussion of movie archive leads us to another question: how many movies have been lost over the 120 years since the first movies were made? The answer is that about 3500 movies are documented as being lost, 90% of which were produced before 1940, and that almost nothing has been lost since 1970 [7]. The industry has become remarkably good at preserving its product [1]. Over 7,000 movies are being made each year[1] and all of them are archived in some way. The lesson we can learn here is that what we tend to lose are the products of early days of a new medium. What is true of movies (most of the loss is pre-1940) is also true of television (most of the loss is pre-1975).

3   Lessons from Movie Production

Let us now turn to consider lessons from production in the movie industry. In particular, lessons that we can learn about creating and maintaining 3D models, such as models of buildings. These artefacts are similar to those that are created and maintained by certain parts of the cultural heritage community.

For this, I draw on the "What's up Prof?" study[2] from December 2008. In that study, a small team of professors visited visual effects and post-production houses in London. Our aim was primarily to discover the challenges they face. We hoped to find computer graphics research problems with which the universities could help. What we found instead was a set of challenging infrastructure problems. Our summary report was published in the February 2010 issue of Leonardo [2]. Here, I provided longer descriptions of those challenges that can be related to cultural heritage. The challenges came in three flavours: technical, infrastructure, and people.

3.1   Technical Issues

Repurposing. Movie companies tend not to re-use existing 3D models. At present, 3D models tend to be made anew for each sequel of a movie. This is understandable as technology moves on between a movie and its sequel. However, we also find that the 3D models used for a movie are not used for the accompanying game. There is thus enormous duplication of effort across time and across different organisations.

This has resonances with 3D in cultural heritage, where each organisation constructs models using their own software, in whatever format is most convenient, with whatever metadata they think necessary. Repurposing this 3D data for other applications can be challenging. The movie industry has tended to avoid doing this at all, which indicates that 3D modelling is not yet mature enough for it to be advantageous to attempt to reuse rather than build from scratch. The CAD industry,

---

[1] Source for 7,000 new movies per year is the Internet Movie Database [8], which reported 6,886 feature films released in 2009, and higher numbers in subsequent years.

[2] For those who miss the cultural reference here: the title "What's up Prof?" is a reference to "What's up doc?", the catch-phrase of the Warner Brothers' cartoon character Bugs Bunny.

by contrast, has faced the problem of multiple data formats for decades. There is an active market for software (e.g., TranscenData's *CADfix*) that accurately converts 3D models between different, often partially-incompatible, formats.

Finding Assets (indexing). An individual movie will now use millions of assets, including 3D models, texture maps, and image layers. Any asset may appear in several different versions. Almost anything that is generated as an intermediate product will also be stored, because it is easier to store it "just in case" than to delete it and then have to rebuild it. A movie will employ hundreds of effects artists making hundred of shots over two or three years. It is vital that those digital assets are well indexed, so that an artist can easily find the correct version of an asset for the particular job at hand. The databases of assets are now so large that we need better ways to search images and 3D models.

These problems are also faced in cultural heritage, with the added disadvantage that we are not aiming for some finished product (the movie), after which we can discard the assets and their index, but rather we need to preserve the assets, their relationships, and a good index for decades. We also need to ensure that our meta-data remains accurate as our database matures.

Metadata Matters. The Academy's case study on archiving digital film underscores the importance of metadata:

> "Archival processing efforts and costs increase exponentially if digital materials are not 'born archival.' That is, metadata should be captured and created at the time of content creation, and organization of materials for archiving should be considered and implemented as part of the production process." [6]

In both movies and cultural heritage applications, it is vital that the metadata is created alongside the object. Generating metadata later is expensive and prone to inaccuracy.

3D Reconstruction. In 2008, the "What's up Prof?" team was told that "reasonable methods" exist for the reconstruction of 3D objects but that they work best with frame-synchronised views from binocular cameras. Support for 3D (stereoscopic) movie-making became a priority for the industry following the popularity of 3D releases like *Avatar* (2009) [9]. This led to high-quality binocular cameras being readily available, and such cameras are expected to bring benefits to cultural heritage by providing cheap, rapid capture of 3D objects. Extraction of point clouds from video or stereoscopic video seems well advanced. Extraction of data of *good enough quality* for the reconstruction of a complete 3D scene from multiple movie cameras is still challenging. As this technology matures, it will become readily applicable to cultural heritage applications.

3.2   Infrastructure Issues

Trans-Coding Media between Digital Formats. There has been a proliferation of formats, which means that, for example, when producing advertisements, a single advert can be required in 10 different formats. To compound this, different subsets of

Table 1. Statistics from the making of *The Tale of Despereaux* (2008)
[provided by Framestore]

Item	Statistic
Number of shots	1713
Number of locations	63
Number of (hero) characters	53
Number of variants in crowds	263
Number of props	1080
Number of 3D models	6098
Crew size (peak)	280
Render farm (CPUs)	4500
On-line data	150 terabytes
Number of published versions of assets	4,031,382
Dependencies between assets	20,375,436
Metadata (number of objects)	29,797,895
Metadata (number of attributes associated with objects)	397,714,992

those 10 will be required for each country in which the advert is used. Further, a contract may be for up to 100 adverts. The net result is that a lot of CPU time and staff time is spent in converting between video formats. Some effects houses have staff whose entire job is to trans-code between formats.

Consider archiving this digital artefact: how many of those formats should be archived? Is there a definitive version that should be stored for posterity? The movie industry has had a traditional policy of "save everything", which is unsustainable [1].

This has resonances in cultural heritage when we generate derivative artefacts. Should there be one master 3D file for a given object? Should we archive the derivatives of that file? What do we do if the original object changes in some way? How many versions do we keep? What is a significant change?

Transmission of Large Quantities of Data Including Backup of Large Data Stores. A post-production or visual effects house will produce gigabytes of new data each day. One company reported that no vendor of off-site backup was able to cope with the quantity of new data that they produce. Two companies commented that, because of this, they maintain their backups on site, with the obvious security risk. Images, video, and 3D models all require a lot of storage space. How much space should we reasonably allocate to them? Who will decide what should be archived, what should be backed-up, and what is ephemeral?

Again, this has resonance with cultural heritage projects, where vast amounts of data can be generated on site. It is important to realise that the film industry still struggles to handle large quantities of data, and it will be useful to get that industry's advice on practical solutions to these serious infrastructure problems.

Keeping Up with Technology. In parts of the industry, the basic algorithms have changed little in the past decade. The key problem faced in these parts of the industry is making best use of new technology to speed up processes and to keep ahead of the competition. For example, one company reported that only 10–20% of their code performed image processing, with the rest of the code being required for data management.

The lesson for cultural heritage is that there is much more to 3D modelling than the algorithms for generating and manipulating the models themselves; there are also considerable challenges in ensuring that we can continue to store, retrieve, use, modify and manipulate those models.

Archiving and Cataloguing Assets. Archiving everything is problematic. If we do archive then cataloguing is important so that we know where to find things. For example, *The Tale of Desperaux*[3] (2008) has 1700 effects shots, with 4 million assets, with variations on those assets producing 10 million identifiable objects (see Table 1). These take up several hundred terabytes. The Academy suggests that this is small for a modern movie; it estimates that a single digital motion picture will generating upwards of two petabytes of data [1]. How do you archive something like this? How do you manage the archive? There are many subsidiary questions within this problem: for example, is it sufficient to store the original imagery and models along with a description of the process to get from those to the final shot?

This is an area in which cultural heritage researchers are likely ahead of the film industry. With tighter budgets and a need to preserve the important material for posterity, the cultural heritage industry has already had to face questions of just what should be stored and in what format.

3.3   People and Process Issues

Managing Artists. Fifteen years ago, the creative 3D artists in the film industry were generally aware of the underlying technology and of the entire pipeline of getting from concept to the finished film. Today, these 3D artists are often less technically knowledgeable. Because the 3D modelling world has become specialised, artists are now able to concentrate on their creative role, but this leaves them with less knowledge of the technical underpinnings of their tools. This leads, inevitably, to situations where they fail to use the full power of the tools or fail to understand the implications of their actions for the later stages of the pipeline. On the other side of the emerging divide are technologists who understand the computer systems but not the ways in which artists work. The film industry greatly values those people who can bridge this divide: those who are experts in one domain, but who understand, respect, and can talk intelligently with those in the other domain.

This has echoes in the cultural heritage arena, where we have experts in complementary disciplines who can easily fail to understand one another. We need expert historians, archaeologist, technologists, and computer scientists. We need to train people who will become expert in one field but who will understand, respect, and be able to talk intelligently with the complementary experts.

Managing a Large Workforce. The film industry once consisted of small companies within which everyone knew everyone else. Over the last decade, several of the

---

[3] *The Tale of Desperaux* is an animated fairy story, produced largely by Framestore in London.

companies have become too large to work in this way. They are struggling with managing a creative, collaborative process when people in different parts of the chain do not know each other and have only a basic understanding of each other's roles.

This is, of course, true of any large organisation that has grown from a small one. If you watch the credits of any modern movie that involves much 3D modelling, you will see hundreds of names scroll past. Producing 3D models has become an intensive business, involving increasingly specialised experts. One cannot expect to do this successfully without good managers to oversee the process.

4   Cooperation between Film Production and Cultural Heritage

Finally, let us consider cooperation between film production and cultural heritage. Naïvely, we might expect there to be substantial scope for mutual benefit between the two. In particular, we might hope that cultural heritage researchers could re-use 3D models that have been created for historical movies.

The movie industry has vast resources and directors often want historical verisimilitude. There is certainly scope for cultural heritage researchers to advise on the historical details of a movie's production. For example, Kathleen Coleman, Professor of Classics at Harvard, was chief academic consultant on Ridley Scott's *Gladiator* (2000). However, she reflects that it is impossible for a single consultant to have an effect on every historical detail [10]. In the case of *Gladiator*, she was only one of over 800 people involved in the movie [8]. Pasinetti makes similar comments on his experience of Mankiewicz's *Julius Caesar* (1953) [11]. Both commentaries are clear that historical consultants play a useful role in such movies; they are not there simply to provide some academic credibility. However, they are also clear that the historical consultant cannot possibly check every detail of a movie.

Given the desire for historical accuracy, it seems sensible to ask whether we can use the movie industry's ability to generate realistic 3D models. For example, could a we arrange for a license to use any 3D models that are created on a movie? This seems a reasonable proposition. The models that are created are of little use to the production house, once the movie is complete, and they have had effort put into them well in excess of what could be funded by an academic project. Compare, for example, the incredible detail in the models in the movie *Gladiator* with the detail that has been possible to include in the academic project, Rome Reborn [12].

Experience of the movie industry indicates that this rosy view of mutually-beneficial work is unlikely to be effective in practice. There are several reasons, most of which reduce to the conflicting aims of the academic researcher and the movie director.

Accuracy *vs* Story-Telling. The academic wants accuracy. The director wants to tell a story. The movie company is paying the bill, so the story-telling takes precedence. If historical accuracy makes for a worse story, historical accuracy will be discarded. In *Gladiator*, the director Ridley Scott wished to produce an historically accurate movie. However, many of the details were altered to make a better story. He comments "I felt the priority was to stay true to the spirit of the period, but not necessarily to adhere to facts. We were, after all, creating fiction, not practicing archaeology." [13]

Winkler highlights this problem in his essay on the movie *Gladiator* [14]: "The appeal of such works rests at least as much on their fictional as on their factual side. Most of the time, the fiction is even more important than the facts because the story being told is what primarily interests us."

For example, the Roman ampitheatre (the Colosseum) was allegedly made larger than real-life because Ridley Scott thought the real one to be too small for the effect he was seeking. There is an irony here: the Colosseum is one of the largest buildings of antiquity. Winkler goes so far as to say that its "...very size and height are proof of Roman hubris." [15] What excess of hubris, then, to require that the movie's version be even larger?

The Impossibility of Accuracy. Where we do not know the historical truth, we have conjectures of various possibilities. Like Schrödinger's Cat, we can hold these in superposition: the truth might have been this or perhaps it was that. A movie, however, must have a definitive version that can be put on screen. The movie's creators must open the box to see whether the cat is alive or dead. Pasinetti, advisor on *Julius Caesar* (1953), comments that "...one crucial difference between scholarship and film making [is that], while the former can afford to be vague in its results, the latter cannot." [11]

Concentration on Hero Buildings. Movies tend to concentrate on spectacle. Much effort will be invested in the big, well-known buildings. If we were to engage in a long-term relationship with the movie studios then, over time, we would end up with several, probably contradictory, models of hero buildings such as the Circus Maximus (e.g., *Ben Hur* (1925)), the Colosseum (e.g., *Gladiator*), the Parthenon, and Tower Bridge (e.g., *Sherlock Holmes* (2009)). Less effort will be invested in the everyday buildings. For example, Weta Digital's reconstruction of 1930s New York for *King Kong* (2005) used procedural modelling for many of the buildings, rather than painstaking hand-crafting [16]. These computer-generated approximations to the true buildings were sufficient for story-telling but would not stand up to scrutiny of the historical detail. The same would be true of a street scene in Pompeii or Athens: so long as it looked reasonable, it would be acceptable, even if it bore only a vague resemblance to what had stood on that street at the purported time of the movie's action. Winkler, again: "If this fiction is based on or embellished by historical or archaeological facts, so much the better, but the appeal of such authenticity is limited. For example, who among the audiences of Cecil B. DeMille's *The Sign of the Cross* (1932) or Mervyn LeRoy's *Quo Vadis* (1951) paid attention to, or remembered afterwards, that most of the décor of these films was highly authentic and had been re-created lovingly and at great expense?" [14]. Coleman puts it more succinctly: "Detail is incidental to plot." [10]

Reference to Earlier Movies. Rather than referring to the historically accurate, movies often refer back to historical inaccuracies of earlier movies. Coleman comments, on the clothing in *Gladiator*: "...the costumes are simultaneously a tribute to the Rome created by Hollywood and an acknowledgement that the Rome that Hollywood created is now the only Rome that is universally familiar." [10]

Concentration on What Can Be Seen. A 3D model for a movie needs only to be visually convincing. Any detail that cannot be seen will not be modelled. Just like a stage set, there is nothing round the back to match what can be seen out the front. This means that a model made for a movie is, at best, just a starting point for a cultural historian. This leads to further problems of finding the staff time to consolidate the model.

File Formats. Finally, we return to a problem we alluded to in Sections 2 and 3. A 3D model for a movie is likely to be constructed in a software environment tailored towards movie making. Exporting that into a software environment tailored for cultural heritage is likely to be difficult, as the requirements of the two environments are likely to have considerable differences.

5   Conclusion

Movies are cultural artefacts in their own right; the preservation of movies gives lessons in the preservation of other ephemera, including all of those digital assets. The particular lesson here is that preservation on physical media should not be idly dismissed as somehow inferior to preservation digitally. There are substantial challenges in the long-term archiving of digital media and often advantages in the careful archiving of physical media.

The film industry requires the management of an enormous number of digital assets, analogous to how digital assets are managed in cultural heritage. The size of the film industry means that they are hitting problems that are faced in cultural heritage, probably before those problems become apparent in the latter field. The economic motivation of the film industry means that they are finding solutions to those problems, or identifying that there is currently no acceptable solution and that a work-around is all that can be done at the present time. Lessons learned here will help researchers in cultural heritage avoid attempts at solving the currently insoluble.

Finally, while collaboration between movie making and cultural heritage seems attractive, the difference in motivation makes it challenging. There is a fundamental tension between wanting scholarly accuracy and wanting to tell a good story.

Acknowlegements. Thanks to the participants at the 2012 EuroMed Workshop on Computational Geometry and Ontologies for Cultural Heritage 3D Digital Libraries who, through discussions at the workshop, contributed many of the ideas on how these lessons apply in cultural heritage. Thanks also to my co-authors on the What's up Prof? project [2]: Dr John Patterson (University of Glasgow) and Prof. Phil Willis (University of Bath).

References

1. Academy of Motion Picture Arts and Sciences: The Digital Dilemma (2007), http://www.oscars.org/science-technology/council/projects/digitaldilemma
2. Dodgson, N.A., Patterson, J., Willis, P.J.: What's up Prof? Current issues in the visual effects and post-production industry. Leonardo 43(1), 92–93 (2010)
3. British Film Institute National Archive, http://www.bfi.org.uk/archive-collections
4. Riley, J.M.: IPI Storage Guide for Acetate Film, Image Permanence Institute (1993), http://acetguid.notlong.com (PDF)
5. HP Ultrium Media QuickSpecs, version 13 DA-11529, http://www.ccidistribution.co.uk/datasheets/2010/apr/LTO.pdf (PDF)
6. Academy of Motion Picture Arts and Sciences: Long-Term Management and Storage of Digital Motion Picture Materials (2010), http://www.oscars.org/science-technology/council/projects/casestudy/ ISBN 978-0-615-39095-6
7. Lost Films, http://lost-films.eu
8. The Internet Movie Database, http://imdb.com
9. Lipton, L.: Digital stereoscopic cinema: the 21st century. Proc. SPIE, vol. 6803 (2008)
10. Coleman, K.C.: The Pedant Goes to Hollywood: The Role of the Academic Consultant. In: Winkler, M.M. (ed.) Gladiator: Film and History, pp. 45–52. Blackwell, Oxford (2004)
11. Pasinetti, P.M.: Julius Caesar: The Role of the Technical Adviser. The Quarterly of Film Radio and Television 8(2), 131–138 (1953)
12. Rome Reborn Video of version 2.2 (August 25, 2011), http://www.youtube.com/watch?v=vrIEwjgfbYs
    Project website: http://www.romereborn.virginia.edu
13. Landau, D. (ed.): Gladiator: The Making of the Ridley Scott Epic. Newmarket Press, New York (2000) cited in [14]
14. Winkler, M.M.: Gladiator and the Traditions of Historical Cinema. In: Winkler, M.M. (ed.) Gladiator: Film and History, pp. 16–30. Blackwell, Oxford (2004)
15. Winkler, M.M.: Gladiator and the Colosseum: Ambiguities of Spectacle. In: Winkler, M.M. (ed.) Gladiator: Film and History, pp. 87–110. Blackwell, Oxford (2004)
16. White, C.: King Kong: The Building of 1933 New York City. In: SIGGRAPH 2006: ACM SIGGRAPH 2006 Sketches, p. 96. ACM, New York (2006)

All links to websites were checked as correct on 14 July 2014.

Reusing Multimedia Content for the Creation of Interactive Experiences in Cultural Institutions

Maria Teresa Linaza, Miriam Juaristi, and Ander Garcia

Dept. of eTourism and Cultural Heritage, Vicomtech, Paseo Mikeletegi 57,
20009 Donostia-San Sebastian, Spain
{mtlinaza,mjuaristi,agarcia}@vicomtech.org

Abstract. Information and Communication Technologies (ICT) have changed the society, including the recreational experiences. ICTs have created new spaces for the recreational participation, which often only recreate the same experiences on virtual spaces. These technological advances are one of the main drivers of the cultural and creative production. As people use ICTs in different activities of their daily life, such as home entertainment, they demand a higher sophistication level in cultural heritage applications. This paper describes the implementation of a software framework to generate cultural experiences, aiming at their integration in current flows of creative processes; semantic standardized access to different distributed knowledge sources; flexible integration of services; and content oriented visualization. It is worth highlighting that this platform will allow users without a technology background (content producers, education departments of cultural institutions) to generate new experiences based on reusing existing multimedia contents and designing the stories they want to tell.

Keywords: Authoring Tool, storytelling, multimedia content, Europeana.

1   Introduction

There are many initiatives to make cultural content available online on the basis of standard easily searchable metadata descriptions. An outstanding example is Europeana that aggregates large amounts of annotated multimedia cultural data. Each heritage piece in this online collection tells a story about why it is significant, what it shows, where it came from and how it relates to other items in the collection and elsewhere. Although huge amounts of resources have been invested in digitization and indexation of the contents, there is still a lack of real-world applications based on reusing multimedia contents coming from large-scale repositories. Thus, there is an urgent need to turn this content into a valuable and coherent experience for users.

On the other hand, the development of multimedia contents has influenced storytelling, an ancient art form where experiences, events and actions are conveyed in words, images and sounds. Traditionally, this art form has been an oral performance with an interactive relation between the storyteller and the audience. A single person (the storyteller) communicates a series of events to a passive audience.

M. Ioannides and E. Quak (Eds.): 3D Research Challenges, LNCS 8355, pp. 104–118, 2014.

The advent of digital contents has given rise to the so-called digital storytelling, a combination of the art of telling stories with a mixture of digital graphics, text, recorded audio narration, video and music to present information on a specific topic.

Although people have written and told stories for thousands of years, digital storytelling partially driven by audience participation has emerged in the last 30 years. Even nowadays, the skills needed to author successful interactive stories are still not well understood, as the experience creators are used to traditional static narratives in print, film and television formats. Interactivity encloses planning many types of interactions with the objects in the experience, making it much more complex to maintain coherence and control over the dynamic story. To author a successful story, the experience creators should have the skills of a creative master and the technical knowledge of the data structures and software tools used for a story engine.

Furthermore, most of the multimedia applications today do not adequately support adaptation to different visualization channels, namely mobile applications, Web-based browsers or gesture-based devices. Many existing authoring tools have been implemented in specific technologies for target situations (for example, mobile devices in a gallery). Thus, content creators and developers must face the challenge of targeting different channels in a cost-effective way.

This paper describes the implementation of the GeneraTour framework to author multichannel cultural experiences, aiming at their integration in current flows of creative processes; semantic standardized access to different distributed knowledge sources; flexible integration of services; and content oriented visualization. It is worth highlighting that this platform will allow users without a technology background (content producers, education departments of cultural institutions, experience creators) to generate new experiences based on existing Europeana multimedia contents and designing the stories they want to tell.

This paper has been structured as following. Sections 2 and 3 describe in detail the two main pillars of the developed framework, namely authoring tools and storytelling in Cultural Heritage. The following section describes the GeneraTour framework. The final section includes some conclusions and future work.

2   Authoring Tools

2.1   Definitions

Bulterman and Hardman (1995) [6] defined an authoring system as "a program that assists the user in managing the creative task of specifying the placement and relative order of media object events". They have categorized authoring tools into four basic approaches:

- Graph-based authoring. This approach uses a schematic diagram of the control flow interactions among multimedia objects.
- Timeline-based authoring. These systems provide a schematic diagram of the dataflow interactions among multimedia objects. A number of events are shown in parallel relative to a common axis.

- Programming-based authoring. Both previous paradigms use graphs and illustrations to describe the interaction among media items in a presentation. In this case, a programming-based system provides low-level facilities to specify the components, their timing, layout and interactions within a presentation.
- Structure-based authoring. This approach separates the definition of the logical structure of a presentation and the media objects associated with a document.

As many of the existing authoring tools, GeneraTour aims at providing a framework for the management and authoring of cultural multimedia assets for non-technical users with limited expertise in the field of computer programming. During the years, several authoring approaches have been implemented with clear differences in their coverage of the workflow process as well as in their user interface concept. This section has categorized such approaches on the basis of the user interaction channel of the experience authored.

2.2   Authoring Tools for Web-Based Exhibitions

Web-based exhibitions have become a common means for cultural institutions to provide access to Cultural Heritage information resources to the public. Authoring and managing a Web-based exhibition can be a tedious and time-consuming task involving a set of skills that may not be available in a cultural institution context. Thus, in order to simplify the creation of such exhibitions, several authoring tools have been developed. All these systems facilitate the development of multiple versions of the same exhibition in different contexts by separating content and presentation.

One example is the ViEx system [5] based on three major components: a content management system; its underlying content database; and a set of layout templates. The content of a ViEx exhibition is organized in a layout-independent way, as building blocks for the experience may be pages, pictures with descriptive information, video, audio, text and panoramas. One of its main disadvantages is the lack of support for metadata.

Costagliola *et al* (2002) [8] presented a formal approach called CREW, specialized in the development of 3D virtual exhibitions of Cultural Heritage. The tool is mainly oriented to the content experts, such as the curator of the exhibition, the art expert, the media expert and the layout designer. The approach provides a set of visual modelling languages tailored to the specification of virtual exhibitions. Such languages have been integrated in an authoring tool which supports the key figures to carry out the tasks on the basis of visual interfaces.

Furthermore, Patel *et al* (2005) [20] developed the ARCO system to create, manipulate, manage and present artefacts in virtual exhibitions, both internally within the museum environment and over the Web. Conceptually, the system includes the three major functions of content production, management and visualization. This system emphasizes creating 3D digital copies of artefacts on the Web, limiting its users to cultural organizations with 3D contents.

Yang, Ramaiah and Foo (2007) [30] developed the VAES framework to create, update, extract and search metadata of artefacts and exhibitions stored in a database. A virtual exhibition is created on the basis of a predefined exhibition and artefact metadata stored in the database. An authoring tool provides a direct manipulation work area for users to browse, display and layout the exhibition page content that is extracted from the database.

More recently, Chittaro et al (2010) [7] implemented a high-level tool to build 3D virtual exhibitions from pre-existing 3D models in order to design virtual visits. The tool provides a 3D interface in first-person view to navigate through the virtual space and arrange exhibits. Artificial Intelligence (AI) techniques allow defining interesting points of view inside the exhibition area. These points can be connected to create a virtual tour. The tool has been used to build the virtual visit of a church with representative Renaissance frescoes.

Finally, the eXhibition:editor3D creates virtual 3D exhibitions from existing digitalized exhibition content like 3D assets, photographs, videos and audioclips [18]. It allows the curators and editors to design and preview upcoming exhibitions; archive temporary exhibitions; create interactive 3D presentations for multimedia terminals; or create catalogues and websites. The editor can organize its content in virtual rooms, so that multiple rooms are combined together within a project to present different exhibition rooms.

2.3   Authoring Tools for Mobile Applications

Mobile devices have gained increasing acceptance as platforms for accessing cultural experiences due to their suitability in this field. Thus, the development of authoring tools for the implementation of mobile applications for cultural institutions has attracted a lot of commercial attention. Generally speaking, current tools for authoring mobile applications are light versions of state-of-the-art commercial multimedia authoring tools. This section reviews two of the most representative ones.

On the one hand, Macromedia Flash Lite is one of the most commonly used multimedia authoring tools that has been used in the implementation of a promotional campaign of the natural history museum of the Petrified forest in Lesvos, Greece [10]. On the other hand, NaviPocket has been designed to develop multimedia guides, especially for PDA. Based on NaviPocket, the "Fables" prototype for the Stratis Eleftheriadis Teriade Museum in Greece uses PDA to provide enriched multimedia interpretative information for the collection of "Fables" by Jean de La Fontaine [16]. Although both tools have accelerated the delivery of advanced applications, they are not Open Source, do not support content maintenance and require Windows compatible devices for the development and run-time.

Further research authoring frameworks have been implemented for the implementation of mobile experiences. For instance, Barrenho et al (2006) [4] describe the InStory project, which has implemented a platform for the development of exploratory geo-referenced activities. Authoring in this project includes creating and geo-referencing the components, associating media content to them and establishing connections between them. Users can retrieve multimedia content on their mobile devices while visiting a cultural, historical or natural Cultural Heritage. Finally, Linaza *et al* (2008) [13] implemented an authoring tool for non-expert users to allow the creator of the guide to decide which contents to include and the languages in which the guide will be provided. This tool has been validated in several archaeological sites in order to build interactive multilingual mobile guides based on the J2ME standard.

2.4   Other Types of Authoring Tools

Natural interaction metaphors in cultural institutions include the impression of handling a real book, or flipping pages using touch-screens or gestures. For instance, the DocExplore research project [27] has implemented a technology-based system for the exploration of historical documents. It includes three main applications: the Manuscript Management Tool to manage and annotate collections of digitized manuscripts; the Authoring Tool to build multimedia presentations of augmented documents; and the Viewer to visualize and interact with multimedia presentations. In this case, the aim of the Authoring Tool is related to the definition of a course through the selection of pages from the existing contents.

As it has been presented in this section, the increasing number of technologies and devices can empower further authoring approaches in the field of Cultural Heritage such as innovative multichannel approaches. For instance, NIPPON-multimedia is a multimedia application developed on the basis of the Instant Multimedia technology to coordinate the production of different experiences optimized for different channels (Web, podcast, iOS applications, SmartPhones) [25]. As in the GeneraTour approach, the simple authoring environment enables the edition of the experience and the definition and selection of multimedia content for each element. The framework produces and publishes the final applications for different delivery channels. The main difference with the GeneraTour approach is the additional interaction means of GeneraTour, such as Kinect-based experiences or the traditional catalogues for cultural exhibitions.

3   Storytelling in Cultural Heritage

As it has been previously defined, storytelling is an ancient way of communication and information flow between people. Traditionally, it is an oral performance with an interactive relation between storyteller and audience. The storyteller often uses a set of fragments of plots that are mixed and composed in a fuzzy way [15]. The most common conception of the story is a linear sequence of scenes, which is very popular in cultural institutions, as this type of storytelling allows presenting stories of artefacts and also people who lived the history. As digital media is the major media nowadays, there are several new types of storytelling. This section provides an overview of different approaches in the storytelling field.

3.1   Digital Storytelling

Digital storytelling combines the art of telling stories with a mix of digital graphics, text, recorded audio narration, video and music to present information on a specific topic [24]. A digital story includes all the elements of traditional stories (setting, plot, conflict, theme, character and point of view), as well as other additional elements such as emotional content to engage the audience, voice and images to illustrate the scripts, or pacing to add emotion to the content. Such stories usually adopt a first person narrative point of view.

The use of digital storytelling has become very popular in virtual heritage applications, as stories about events and characters have been added to many projects related to virtual reconstructions. The form of digital storytelling goes from simple text or audio narration to virtual or real storytellers. For instance, Huseinovic and Turcinhodzic (2013) [12] presented a story-guided cultural heritage environment, where the visitor is guided through the virtual museum to present intangible cultural heritage such as legends, tales, poems, rituals or dances. The virtual reconstruction has been first implemented as a computer animation rendered in a movie.

3.2   Collaborative Storytelling

A story can be created individually or by a group. The members of a group (distributed or in the same place) may collaborate on the creation of a story, which can be done synchronously or asynchronously using different media [23]. This collaborative storytelling enables building social interactions and facilitating communication among the members of a community. Collaborative storytelling often takes place in a co-narration form [20], in which participants communicate and exchange ideas orally to generate ideas to build stories.

One of the first approaches in collaborative storytelling has been the linear platform that provides a collaborative space in which participants remix stories using a linear approach. Such stories have exactly one beginning, one middle and one end. Examples include Dramatica [23], CBC4Kids [3] and Lizzy [9]. In such linear platforms, no other story branches are possible.

Digital storytelling can address groups in ways that would not be possible without technology. For example, it can provide individuals in a group with different points of view of a story at the same time, adapting to the behaviour of the group as a whole, rather than just individual behaviour. As an example, TellStory is a Web application that supports the collaborative building of stories [22]. One of the most important issues of TellStory consists in the possibility of the user to use a template in order to address the elaboration of the story through the typical characteristics of a narrative structure.

Finally, StoryMapper is a group-based approach in which the collaboration process is guided by user roles such as teller, organizer or listener [1]. The graphical interface is based on conceptual maps, so that media can be attached to them.

3.3   Interactive Storytelling

One of its main disadvantages is that traditional storytelling does not allow people to interact or alter the plot as users may like. Due to the emergence of information technologies, the cultural and creative industry has begun to explore computational approaches for creating interactive story experiences. Glasner (2004) [11] defined interactive storytelling as a two-way experience, where "the audience member actually affects the story itself". Furthermore, Miller (2008) [17] defined digital storytelling as narrative entertainment that reaches the audience via digital technology and media. Developing interactive narrative experiences is a research subject within different fields, including digital media, artificial intelligence and Human Computer Interaction.

The framework of interactive storytelling is different from the conventional linear story, as the former is a form of non-linear storytelling. While the story begins at one end and goes through a pre-defined sequence to finish at the other end in a linear story, non-linear stories consist of a graph of multiple story "nodes" where each "node" is connected to one or more other "nodes". The connections between these "nodes" represent possible directions the story might take and the branching from one "node" to the next can either be random or based on some sort of interaction rules.

The existing approaches varied across different works. The first published interactive storytelling software that was widely recognized was Façade [14]. The project combines voice acting and a 3D environment as well as natural language processing and other advanced artificial intelligence techniques for robust interactive storytelling.

A further approach named The Virtual Tour Guide provides information to the visitor on the basis of interactive storytelling techniques [26]. Rather than following a predefined tour that is the same for all visitors, the visitor is allowed to make choices to develop the tour and story. The information is segmented in small and easily-understood information pieces that can be combined according to the choices and preferences of the visitor that are stored in the profile and constantly updated by the visitor tracking. The result is a personalized tour.

Moreover, Tuck and Kuksa (2009) [28] describe the Virtual Heritage Tours project about the Cultural Heritage of Nottingham. Users can choose the road they will take, move around and sometimes interact with the action. The narratives are triggered as users approach an object. Finally, Adabala *et al* (2010) [2] have implemented a platform to create interactive narratives on the basis of tangible and intangible heritage elements. The framework enables the creator to compose an interactive narrative that conveys the richness of the information while preserving the relationships among different artefacts that take part in the story.

GeneraTour combines different multimedia contents from distributed heterogeneous databases into a single compelling narrative that could be explored in multiple visualization channels.

4   The GeneraTour Platform

4.1   Main Objectives

GeneraTour is an authoring framework to generate multimedia experiences for cultural organizations, which allows both the management and curation of experiences, and the visualization and experimentation by the final user. Experience creators are provided with a narrative space in which they can add, edit and delete narrative contents. Moreover, as experiences are stored and accessed online, they can be edited and updated in real-time.

One of the main advantages of the framework is the split of the authoring in the strict sense (text, images and audio creation and management) from the generation of specific visualization applications, generally developed for specific devices. Generating such one-channel applications means shaping the interface and the interaction mechanisms, selecting the content, adapting and organizing them into an experience structure.

This limitation has been overcome by the GeneraTour framework, which allows building multichannel experiences with the same authoring tool. A middleware to interpret and execute standard formats on all types of visualization platforms defined for GeneraTour has been implemented. In such a way, the authoring framework generates a single representation of an experience that is shared among different visualization environments (author-once approach).

Finally, it is worth highlighting that this platform will allow users without a technology background (content producers, education departments of cultural institutions) to generate new experiences based on reusing existing multimedia contents and designing the stories they want to tell.

4.2   Technical Description

The front end of the Authoring Tool is a HTML5 and JavaScript Web application based on a Rich Internet Application (RIA) architecture following a Model-View Controller (MVC) design pattern. On the other hand, the back-end runs on a Java server with Apache Web Server and Apache Tomcat. The Authoring Tool includes four main building blocks that represent each of the steps in the authoring process, as shown in Fig. 1.

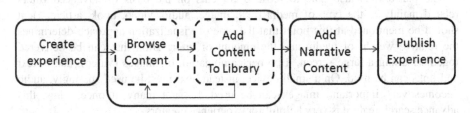

Fig. 1. Work flow of the authoring process

Step 1 is related to the creation or uploading of an experience (Fig. 2). When creating a new experience, the content creator must select the title of the experience as well as the visualization and interaction channel. Five types of channels have been defined for the prototype, such as KinectExperience (gesture-based interaction with Kinect devices over large screens); MobileExperience (Web applications for mobile devices); MuseumExperience (catalogues and other traditional media in exhibitions); WebExperience (Web applications for desktop computers or kiosks) and TourismExperience (Web applications for mobile devices that include geo-located information and Layar-based Augmented Reality features). The creator can also select and load existing experiences (for example, the Euromed experience).

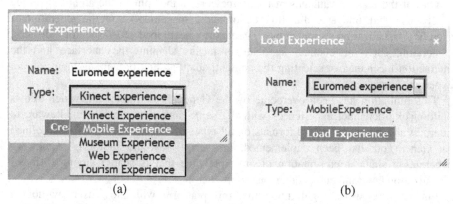

(a)   (b)

Fig. 2. Graphical interface for: (a) creating a new experience, including the definition of the visualization channel; (b) uploading an existing experience

In step 2, creators can navigate and browse through heterogeneous multimedia resources coming from their own institution or external knowledge databases. In order to demonstrate the scalability of the prototype, the platform currently includes two main external data sources: Europeana, accessible through its own API in read-only mode, and Euskomedia, a local database for Basque contents from where contents are imported and duplicated in the GeneraTour database. The performance is direct, as it is enough to introduce the keywords and select the content. Fig. 3 displays the results of a query based on the keyword Picasso. As the query is very generic, more than 298 pages with multimedia contents (image, video, audio) have been retrieved.

The platform is also able to retrieve contents on the basis of advanced filters related mainly to the type of media (text, image, audio, video, book, article,...). It should be mentioned at this point that the type of visualization approach determines the relative weight of media and the amount of information that can be delivered together. Using a large screen, a proper combination of images (video), audio, text and links can be used. On a small device, instead, text must be used sparingly, audio becomes very important, images can be used, but not many at once. Thus, this advance search feature is very helpful for experience creators.

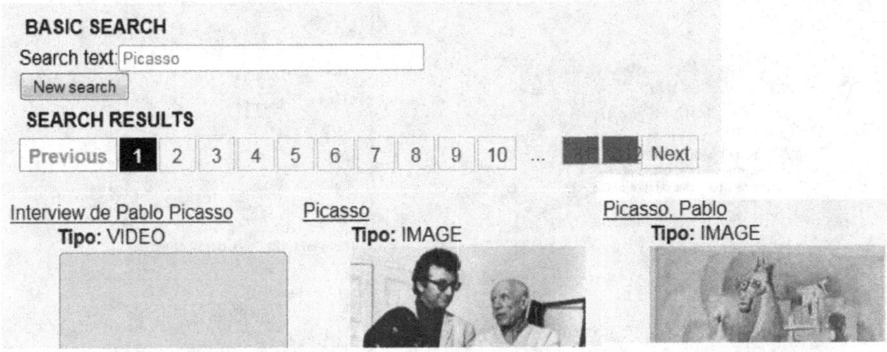

Fig. 3. Graphical interface for browsing and selecting contents from Europeana and other Open Data cultural repositories

When clicking on the content, the creator accesses the corresponding metadata. GeneraTour stores the metadata associated to the multimedia contents selected by the experience creator in the so-called "experience library" (Fig. 4). Such contents are stored as instances of E73.Information_Object class of the CIDOC-CRM ontology. Properties of the instances are automatically initialized with the information available from the data source (Europeana or Euskomedia). In all cases, the experience creator is responsible of analyzing the copyright of the contents in order to check their property rights.

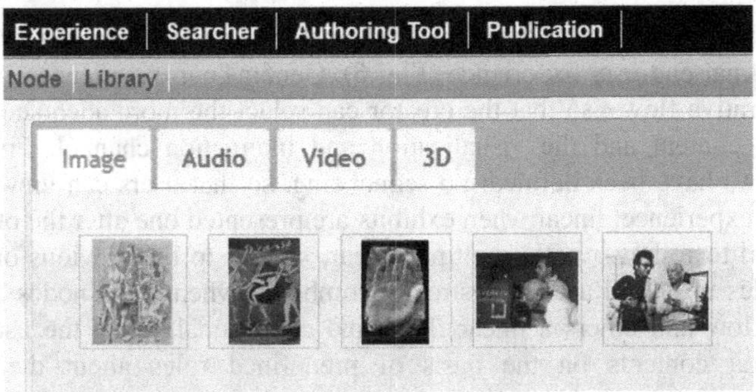

Fig. 4. Selected multimedia contents stored in the "experience library"

In step 3, experience creators are provided with a drag&drop based interface to add, edit and delete narrative content. The platform allows defining several nodes to create an experience. Each node representing a scene of the experience, includes different multimedia contents, such as the title, the text that will be displayed, pictures, video and 3D graphics (Fig. 5). In the case of tourism guides, the creator will add location data for georeferencing.

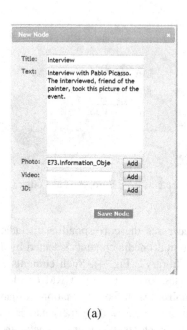

(a)   (b)

Fig. 5. Creating the storytelling of the experience using the Authoring Tool. (a) Description of each node including the multimedia contents; (b) Node with location data.

Once all the nodes are defined, the relationships among them can be defined to achieve the final end-user experience (Fig. 6). GeneraTour experiences are based on different narrative flows, so that the creator can select the more adequate one on the basis of the content and the visualization and interaction channel. Five different narrative flows have been defined: no sequencing, so that users can view any of the nodes of the experience; linear when exhibits are presented one after the other and the user is forced to follow a path; multiple linear, similar to the previous one but with multiple nodes upstream and downstream; combined when some nodes follow a no sequencing flow and others a linear flow; and conditional, when the user can only access several contents on the basis of predefined rules about the previously experienced nodes.

Once the experience is completely defined, the creator can publish it. The output of the authoring tool is a compressed .zip file (step 4) including several files in JSON format that describe the information for each node; the relationships among the nodes; and the type of experience (mobile, Web-based, Kinect-based). Furthermore, multimedia contents (text, video, pictures and 3D objects) associated to each of the nodes are also included in the file. Remote multimedia contents files are retrieved in real-time before the publication of the experience.

If the experience is to be consumed as a Web application (MobileExperience, WebExperience, TourismExperience), the output .zip file will be the input of a Web REST service that will generate a HTML5 Website. This Website will be automatically published on a Web server, sending back the URL of that Website (Fig. 7).

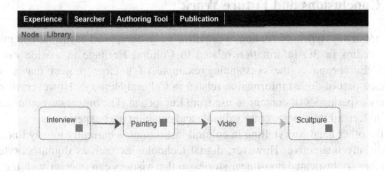

Fig. 6. Linking the nodes of the experience.

Fig. 7. Visualization of the experience in an Android mobile device

Were the experience gesture-based (KinectExperience), the .zip file will also contain the input of a Web REST service that will generate a HTML5 Website compatible with the Microsoft Kinect device. This Kinect-based experience includes three main movements of the hand of the user as a first approach to evaluate the acceptance of the visitors to cultural institutions. Starting with an open hand, users will be able to wave their hand from left to right to go to the next page and from right to left to go back to the last page. The main advantage of the proposed solutions is that the experiences only require a Web browser to run, so that the Kinect device can be installed in any standard desktop computer.

5   Conclusions and Future Work

There are many types of textual, geometric or geographical information, images, videos, audios or 3D information related to Cultural Heritage in a wide range of formats. Europeana is the outstanding example of a large project that stores a significant part of digital information related to Cultural Heritage. However, there are not many experiences of content re-use from Europeana. The bigger current challenge is how to turn all this content into valuable and coherent user experiences.

On the other hand, storytelling in cultural institutions is currently mostly linear and only partially interactive. However, digital technologies such as digital storytelling allow more sophisticated non-linear stories so that visitors can interact with the story at different points in time. Such technologies have a great potential for increasing entertainment for visitors to cultural institutions as they can communicate the heritage in an interactive way.

An Authoring Tool to create interactive multichannel experiences for cultural institutions on the basis of existing multimedia contents has been described in this paper. GeneraTour supports experience creators when developing narrative structures to describe objects and stories of an exhibition. The narrative elements or nodes are re-orderable and editable, so that new nodes can be easily added. Furthermore, the authoring tool can create multichannel experiences from an exhibition, for catalogues and handouts, for online viewing or within a museum space, for mobile applications or for advanced interaction techniques such as Kinect.

The current version of the framework can be considered to be ready for a more formal evaluation. Thus, a formal evaluation of the GeneraTour project is planned in the forthcoming months in order to provide feedback on the usability of the system and on the identification of the main problems encountered.

References

1. Acosta, C.E., Collazos, C.A., Guerrero, L.A., Pino, J.A., Neyem, H.A., Motelet, O.: StoryMapper: a multimedia tool to externalize knowledge. In: 24th International Conference of the Chilean Computer Science Society, pp. 133–140. IEEE Computer Society, Los Alamitos (2004)
2. Adabala, N., Datha, N., Joy, J., Kulkarni, C., Manchepalli, A., Sankar, A., Walton, R.: An Interactive Multimedia Framework for Digital Heritage Narratives. Technical Report, Microsoft Research MSR-TR-2010-101 (2010)
3. Antle, A.: Case study: the design of CBC4Kids' storybuilder. In: 2003 Conference on Interaction Design and Children, pp. 59–68. ACM Press, Preston (2003)
4. Barrenho, F., Romão, T., Martins, T., Correia, N.: InAuthoring environment: interfaces for creating spatial stories and gaming activities. In: 2006 ACM SIGCHI International Conference on Advances in Computer Entertainment Technology. ACM, New York (2006)
5. Breiteneder, C., Platzer, H.: A re-usable software framework for authoring and managing web exhibitions,
http://www.archimuse.com/mw2001/papers/breiteneder/breitened
er2.html

6. Bulterman, D.C.A., Hardman, L.: Multimedia authoring tools: State of the art and research challenges. In: van Leeuwen, J. (ed.) Computer Science Today. LNCS, vol. 1000, pp. 575–591. Springer, Heidelberg (1995)

7. Chittaro, L., Ieronutti, L., Ranon, R., Siotto, E., Visintini, D.: A High-Level Tool for Curators of 3D Virtual Visits and its Application to a Virtual Exhibition of Renaissance Frescoes. In: 11th International Symposium on Virtual Reality, Archaeology and Intelligent Cultural Heritage, pp. 147–154. Eurographics Association, Aire-la-Ville (2010)

8. Costagliola, G., Di Martino, S., Ferrucci, F., Pittarello, F.: An approach for authoring 3D cultural heritage exhibitions on the web. In: 14th International Conference on Software Engineering and Knowledge Engineering, pp. 601–608. ACM, New York (2002)

9. Désilets, A., Paquet, S.: Wiki as a tool for web-based collaborative story telling in primary school: a case study. In: World Conference on Educational Multimedia, Hypermedia and Telecommunications 2005, pp. 770–777. AACE, Chesapeake (2005)

10. Economou, D., Gavalas, D., Kenteris, M.: Authoring tools & development platforms: Requirements for mobile devices-enabled cultural applications. In: 11th Panhellenic Conference on Informatics, pp. 419–432. New Technologies Publications, Athens (2007)

11. Glassner, A.: Interactive Storytelling. A. K. Peters (2004)

12. Huseinovic, M., Turcinhodzic, R.: Interactive animated storytelling in presenting intangible cultural heritage. In: 17th Central European Seminar on Computer Graphics, pp. 65–72. Vienna University of Technology, Vienna (2013)

13. Linaza, M.T., Torre, I., Beusing, R., Tavernise, A., Etz, M.: Authoring tools for archaeological mobile guides. In: 9th International conference on Virtual Reality, Archaeology and Cultural Heritage, pp. 47–54. Eurographics Association, Aire-la-Ville (2008)

14. Mateas, M., Stern, A.: Facade: An experiment in building a fully-realized interactive drama. In: Game Developer's Conference 2003 (2003)

15. McKee, R.: Story: Substance, Structure, Style and the Principles of Screenwriting. Harper Collins Publisher, New York (1998)

16. Micha, K., Economou, D.: Using Personal Digital Assistants (PDAs) to Enhance the Museum Visit Experience. In: Bozanis, P., Houstis, E.N. (eds.) PCI 2005. LNCS, vol. 3746, pp. 188–198. Springer, Heidelberg (2005)

17. Miller, C.: Digital Storytelling. Elsevier (2008)

18. Möstl, R., Hecher, M., Derler, C., Eggeling, E., Fellner, D.W.: Tangible Culture-Designing Virtual Exhibitions on Multi Touch. ERCIM News 86, 21–22 (2011)

19. Norrick, N.R.: Twice-told tales: collaborative narration of familiar stories. Language in Society 26(2), 199–220 (2009)

20. Patel, M., White, M., Mourkoussis, N., Walczak, K., Wojciechowski, R., Chmielewski, J.: Metadata requirements for digital museum environments. International Journal on Digital Libraries 5, 179–192 (2005)

21. Peponis, J., Dalton, R., Wineman, J., Dalton, N.: Path, theme and narrative in open plan exhibition settings. In: Fourth International Space Syntax Symposium, London, pp. 1–20 (2003)

22. Perret, R., Borges, M.R.S., Santoro, F.M.: Applying Group Storytelling in Knowledge Management. In: de Vreede, G.-J., Guerrero, L.A., Marín Raventós, G. (eds.) CRIWG 2004. LNCS, vol. 3198, pp. 34–41. Springer, Heidelberg (2004)

23. Phillips, M.A., Huntley, C.: Dramatica: a Theory of Story,
http://www.dramatica.com/theory/theory_book/dtb.html

24. Robin, B.R.: The Educational Uses of Digital Storytelling. University of Houston (2006)

25. Rubegni, E., Di Blas, N., Paolini, P., Sabiescu, A.: A format to design narrative multimedia applications for cultural heritage communication. In: 2010 ACM Symposium on Applied Computing, pp. 1238–1239. ACM, New York (2010)
26. Song, M., Elias, T., Martinovic, I., Mueller-Wittig, W., Chan, T.K.Y.: Digital heritage application as an edutainment tool. In: ACM SIGGRAPH International Conference on Virtual Reality Continuum and its Applications in Industry, pp. 163–167. ACM, New York (2004)
27. Tranouez, P., Nicolas, S., Dovgalecs, V., Burnett, A., Heutte, L., Liang, Y., Guest, R., Fairhurst, M.: DocExplore: overcoming cultural and physical barriers to access ancient documents. In: ACM Symposium on Document Engineering, pp. 205–208. ACM, New York (2012)
28. Tuck, D., Kuksa, I.: Virtual Heritage Tours: Developing Interactive Narrative-Based Environments for Historical Sites. In: Iurgel, I.A., Zagalo, N., Petta, P. (eds.) ICIDS 2009. LNCS, vol. 5915, pp. 336–339. Springer, Heidelberg (2009)
29. Wolff, A., Mulholland, P., Collins, T.: Storyspace: a story-driven approach for creating museum narratives. In: 23rd ACM Conference on Hypertext and Social Media, pp. 79–88. ACM, New York (2012)
30. Yang, R., Ramaiah, C.K., Foo, S.: Virtual archival exhibition system: an authoring tool for developing web-based virtual exhibitions. In: 2007 International Conference on Dublin Core and Metadata Applications: Application Profiles: Theory and Practice, pp. 96–105. Dublin Core Metadata Initiative, Dublin (2007)

3D Printing for Cultural Heritage: Preservation, Accessibility, Research and Education

Moritz Neumüller[1], Andreas Reichinger[2], Florian Rist[3], and Christian Kern[3]

[1] Artecontacto Kunstvermittlung, Vienna, Austria
touch@artecontacto.org
[2] VRVis Forschungs-GmbH, Vienna, Austria
reichinger@vrvis.at
[3] Institute for Art and Design, Vienna University of Technology, Vienna, Austria
frist@fs.tum.de, chkern@mail.tuwien.ac.at

Abstract. Additive manufacturing, if seconded by a paradigm change to the museum model, can be employed in many ways to reintegrate touch, and other non-retinal senses into our cultural experiences. These multi-sensorial forms of experiencing culture also have a great benefit for the accessibility of cultural heritage, especially for persons with learning difficulties, for children, the elderly, for blind or visually impaired visitors. 3D Printing is in a phase of rapid technological changes and promises more enhancing experiences for the field of cultural heritage. This would provide a more holistic appreciation of the produced objects, but make it necessary to develop basic guidelines for 3D printed models. We expect that 3D Printing will not only become vital in the field of reconstruction of objects, but also for research, documentation, preservation and educational purposes, and it has the potential to serve these purposes in an accessible and all-inclusive way.

Keywords: 3D Printing, Cultural Heritage, Preservation, Accessibility, Education, Models, Reliefs, Museums, Rapid Prototyping, Additive Manufacturing, Design For All.

1 Introduction

Today, a rising interest for multi-sensory experiences, such as touch, smell, and sound[1], coincides with the promise of 3D Printing to transform our contemporary lives, and to foster "a new industrial revolution" [1]. Apart from the industrial and commercial use, there is a fast-growing community of people who use Rapid Prototyping to produce things in small numbers at home, using peer-to-peer networks to exchange their prototypes and designs. At the same time, we see the introduction of (purely visual) 3D into the consumer market as well, namely stereoscopic television screens, photo frames, games and tablets.

---

[1] Elkins points out that "seeing is embodied, and it should no longer be separated from touching, feeling, and from the full range of somatic response", yet he also asks for a more rigorous way when thinking about this materiality [3, p. 25ff].

M. Ioannides and E. Quak (Eds.): 3D Research Challenges, LNCS 8355, pp. 119–134, 2014.
© Springer-Verlag Berlin Heidelberg 2014

It is in this context that we would like to explore the possibilities of 3D Printing in the field of cultural heritage, and *culture* in general. Rapid Prototyping promises a more enhancing experience of 3D models, even if the majority of 3D printers can only print with a limited color-scheme and have little versatility in materials. Yet, it should be a mere question of time until more powerful full-color 3D printers will enter the realms of artistic production and cultural heritage, and it seems not out of reach that they will be able to represent characteristics such as texture, weight and smell or me-chanical characteristics [2], which would provide a more holistic appreciation of the produced objects.

2   Material Turn and Multi-sensory Experiences in the Art Field

In recent years, we have seen a reconsideration of traditional categories within the art field, for example, concerning the term *Plastic Arts*, which had been largely substi-tuted by *Visual Arts*. This replacement is much more than a simple word-game, as it has pushed Plastic Arts into the realm of craftsmanship, and eliminated all connota-tions of multisensory experiences, which are necessary for a full appreciation of a work of art. In the Encyclopedia Britannica's entry on *Visual Art*, we find that the term includes "two-dimensional visual arts such as drawing and painting and also three-dimensional visual arts such as sculpture and architecture". Interestingly enough, the entry continues by immediately restricting the purely *visual* character of these art forms: "Some of these should doubtless be called visuo-tactual art: buildings are ordinarily touched as well as seen, sculptures could be more fully appreciated if touched as well as seen, and even paintings may sometimes have enough three-dimensionality to repay touch experience." [4]

This careful attention to the tactile aspects of the medium, especially in its recep-tion, shows the difficulty of the term Visual Art, which came into use in the 1940s, in the modernist debate about the limits and unique qualities of the different art forms.[2] Consequently, the term *Plastic* Arts, which used to include art forms such as painting, sculpture, drawing and architecture was generally substituted by the concept of *Visual* Arts. The decade of the 1980s has been crucial in this shift, significantly coinciding with the invention of Graphic User Interfaces, the birth of MTV, and an unseen boom in the art market.

This "visualism" [6] in terminology goes hand in hand with a "virtualization" of the cultural field, as the digital revolution has profoundly changed the artistic practice [7] and research methods in Art History, Archeology and in the Cultural Heritage domain in general. Media Art forms in the late 20th century hardly involved any phys-ical manipulation of a plastic medium or physical support. This virtualization of the arts, strongly paralleled with the vast changes in our "real world", has radically driven

---

[2] In his seminal article *Towards a Newer Laocoon* [5], the American art critic addresses the longstanding question of the limits that serve to distinguish between the various artistic dis-ciplines.

back all other sensory channels. Especially olfaction, thermoception, balance and tactile input, once fundamental to understand a work of art, have been eliminated or translated into visual information.

Since the turn of the century, however, *Post-Medium* [8] and *Post-Media* Theory [9] reflect the decline of the Greenbergian concept of medium-specificity, and recent approaches to art theory [10, 11] show a new interest in tactility and the physical aspects of the artwork. Art education backs this "material turn" with its new practice of interactivity, sensorial experiences and hands-on learning in the museum context [12]. In fact, the practice of touching, of being able to hold an object in your hands, had only been abandoned in the early nineteenth century: "In contrast to the multi-sensory modes of previous centuries, in the 1800s sight was increasingly considered to be the only appropriate sense for aesthetic appreciation for 'civilized' adults" [6, p. 207]. The Victorian age was "an era of rising visualism in many ways", and gave birth to a new art consumption and museum model, which was now based on a "Please Do Not Touch" character. Soon, the habits of "good manners" were fortified with scientific and conservational arguments: Given that our hands are unsterile, non-acid-free and clumsy appendages, they were banned from all museums and even outdoor monuments.

The problem is, we all love to touch and many visitors *need* to use all of their senses in order to perceive art and cultural heritage; especially persons with learning difficulties, children, and blind, or partially sighted visitors. The possibility to touch exhibits and the availability of guided touch tours can help these art lovers to enjoy works of art, sometimes with, most times without having to wear gloves. However, there are things that cannot be understood by touch that easily, especially objects that are too big, too small, too fragile, or have too little haptic information. Simple tactile diagrams [13], together with a well-made audio description, can translate the content of paintings, photographs, video stills, building façades, archaeological sites, or images from a microscope. Hand-made reliefs, as well as CNC-milled replicas are even more engaging than such raised line diagrams. However, it is the advent of Rapid Prototyping, and especially 3D Printing, which has the potential of changing the landscape of multisensory experiences in the field of cultural heritage.

3   Applications of 3D Printing in the Context of Cultural Heritage and Museums

Additive manufacturing, if seconded by a paradigm change to the museum model, can be employed in many ways to reintegrate touch, and other non-retinal senses into our cultural experiences. Cultural heritage researchers have been working with virtual models and augmented reality for many years [14]. To print out the results in order to understand them better is the next logical step, because multisensory experiences lead to a better comprehension [15]. In fact, touching an object means understanding and remembering it better[3].

Some languages back this general perception in a quite natural manner. In German, for example, *begreifen* (to understand), derives from *greifen* (to grab). The same is true for *comprehension*, especially in Romance languages, and to some extent, with the English *grasp*, which is used for haptic and intellectual appropriation.

Fig. 1. Tactile Model of a steel converter made for the Vienna Museum of Technology, in collaboration with VRVis, artecontacto and the Vienna University of Technology

Of course, meaningful haptic experiences heavily depend on the question of scale, which is the basis for all kinds of steering and manipulation mechanisms, be it for micro-surgery or piloting a Jumbo Jet plane. Rapid Prototyping has the ability to bring things to a human scale, which means that tactile models have to fit in our hands, and details have to be adapted to the size of our fingers. Yet, there are still no binding standards for the accessibility and educational value of tactile models. Those prototypes that are made for blind or visually impaired users mostly get some individual testing with a small sample from that target group. However, it would be important to develop some general guidelines for 3D printed tactile models, based on the Design For All approach[4]. A model to follow could be the guidelines developed by

---

[3] Katherine J. Kuchenbecker's research on *Haptography*, that is the recording of tactile experiences, is based on the importance of the sense of touch for our comprehension [16].

[4] Design for All, Universal Design, Inclusive Design or User-centred Design can all be defined as designing and producing goods and services in a way which respects individual differences, taking into account the changes which take place during a lifetime and preserves resources for future generations, so that anyone can access and benefit from all that society offers under comparable conditions. According to the Design for All approach, two simple principles should be taken into consideration: to make the use of products and services easier for everyone, and to ensure that the needs, wishes and expectations of users are taken into consideration in the design and evaluation processes of products or services. [17]

the Art Beyond Sight Foundation for artists who work with raised line diagrams in the context of art or by the North American Braille Authorities for tactile graphics [13, 39]. As Alastair Somerville has put it on his *Acuity Design* blog, "the real benefits of 3d scanning, modeling and printing come when we realize that they enable us to manipulate objects to any shape or scale we wish to enhance meaning" [18].

We expect that 3D Printing will not only become vital in the field of reconstruction of objects, but also for research, documentation, preservation and educational purposes, and it has the potential to serve these purposes in an accessible and all-inclusive way. The vast range of possible applications have consequently been structured into four sections, without any claim of being complete, especially in a phase when technology is changing rapidly.

3.1   Reconstruction and Preservation

The recreation of a Temple Lion for the Harvard's Semitic Museum is a good example for how 3D Printing can be used for reconstruction and preservation of cultural heritage. It seems that originally, two ceramic lions flanked the image of the goddess Ishtar in the temple of the ancient city of Nuzi (today's archaeological site of Yorghan Tepe in Iraq). One of them is quite well preserved, the other one only in fragments. The project will thus blend fragments of the fragmented statue held by the museum in Harvard with pieces created through 3D scans of its nearly intact mirror image, which is kept at the Pennsylvania Museum of Archaeology and Anthropology[5]. The Semitic Museum hired an outside contractor, Learning Sites Inc., to reconstruct the object via photogrammetry[6] and to produce a physical reproduction, which was carried out, apparently, in a combination of 3D Printing and CNC milling, "providing the Semitic Museum with a complete lion so that visitors can appreciate how their pieces would have looked in sculptural context." [19]

Another work-in-progress project in this direction is PhD student Fangjin Zhang's "formalized approach tailored specifically to the restoration of historic artifacts" from the Forbidden City in Beijing, such as an enclosure of a pavilion in the Emperor Chanlong Garden. Zhang's approach consists in "capturing the object in digital 3D form, using laser or optical scanners, and then repairing the digital model before 3D printing the replica" [20].

Cornell University's ambitious *3D Printing of Cuneiform Tablets* project is run by Natasha Gangjee, Hod Lipson, and David I. Owen. The idea is to 3D print Cornell's collection of nearly 10,000 cuneiform tablets from ancient Mesopotamia "to create physical replicas of the tablets that look and feel almost exactly like the originals". Prototypes are made from VRML files using ZCorp's powder-based ink-jet printers with the aim of "matching the look of the original tablets in color and texture" [21].

The next steps in the project will consist of systematically reproducing the cuneiforms from the collection and of "exploring additional methods for scanning and manufacturing cuneiforms at higher resolutions appropriate for reproducing the fine details on the smaller tablets" [21].

---

[5] Object Number: 31-40-1, at the Univ. of Pennsylvania Museum of Archaeology and Anthropology, http://www.penn.museum/collections/object/65906

[6] A "3D PDF" is available on Learning Sites' webpage [19].

Fig. 2. 3D Printed cuneiform tablets from Cornell University. Left: Enlarged (×2) 3D printed reproduction; Middle: original size reproduction (produced on Objet printer); Right: original size reproduction (produced on ZCorp ZPrinter 650). Source: [21].

3.2   Accessibility and Education

Another application for 3D Printing in this context is to provide multi-sensory access to objects that cannot be touched, either for conservation reasons, or because they are too big (e.g., the steel converter in Fig. 1), or too small to understand. Objects that do not have any tactile information beforehand (e.g., images) can be translated or enhanced for a more complete understanding [22]. While physical models "have been shown to enhance learning in general student populations", they are also "indispensable tools for teaching the visually impaired and those with spatial reasoning difficulties" [15, p.3]. However, the high cost of these physical models combined with the decreasing cost of simulation and visualization software and computer modeling have steered educators away from physical models.

The already notable decrease of costs for 3D Printing and its expected general availability could turn this situation around. Furthermore, the past years have seen a paradigm change in the appreciation of multi-sensory experiences in education and culture, and a better understanding of how to integrate people with disabilities[7] in the cultural (and social) context in order to foster their artistic practice. This holistic approach to disability is based on the so-called social model of disability, which sees the issue of "disability" as a socially created problem, as opposed to a medical one, the

---

[7] While language and terminology are continually debated and open to change, *people with disabilities* is currently the term most widely used and accepted by the disability community in many English-speaking countries, the emphasis being on the person ahead of the disability. In Britain, however, *disabled people* is the preferred term, the emphasis being on the disabling of people through the physical, institutional, systemic, economic and attitudinal barriers that society creates rather than on an individual's disability/impairment [23].

"impairment". As arts and culture are opened to these "new" publics, the need for an anthropocentric approach and inclusive, non-discriminating art is growing. Clearly there will not be one "best solution" to the problem of inclusivity in the arts and cultural heritage. Rather, there will be medium-specific solutions, and a strong need to integrate the Design For All philosophy [17] in the practical implementations.

3D Printing can thus be expected to play a crucial part in the accessible and all-inclusive education in cultural heritage, as educators will become increasingly aware of its potential and begin integrating it into the classroom. In the museum context, too, 3D Printing has the potential to become a standard technology for exhibition design, educational efforts and accessibility matters. Needless to say that visitors with visual impairments benefit most from tactile reproductions and interactive installations, but so do children, the elderly and – in fact – the general public as a whole.

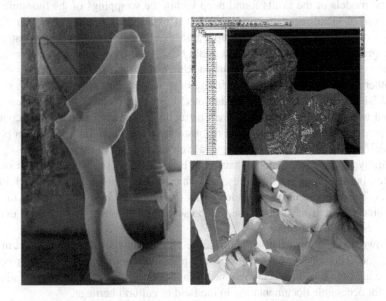

Fig. 3. Untitled photograph by Lotte Hendrich-Hassmann, 1982 / Point cloud as result of a full-body scan and 3D printed plaster model by Florian Rist (Vienna University of Technology), approx. 30 cm high, 2010 / Model used by a blind museum visitor in a touch tour

3.3   Documentation and Research

Already a few years ago, the Smithsonian Institution started to scan and print models from its collection, which can be exhibited at museums, schools and other places to enable more people to have access to them. This makes sense, as only 2% of the Smithsonian's 137 million items are available to the public at any one time. As part of the project, Red Eye on Demand, an outside prototyping company, created a 3D printed replica of a Thomas Jefferson statue, which was installed in an exhibit at the

National Museum of African American History and Culture [24]. A YouTube video published by the Smithsonian in May 2013 explains that "whether it is a rare orchid, a historic gunboat or an archeological site, we see a huge potential to discover and diffuse knowledge [and want to] apply this technology to the Smithsonian at a larger scale" [25]

Another interesting project in the realm of research was the creation of 3D models of three Egyptian busts, which was accomplished by scanning mummies at Redpath Museum in Montreal, Canada. Three human mummies (RM2717, RM2718, & RM2720) from the Redpath Museum at McGill University were scanned using computed tomography at the Montreal Neurological Institute as part of a collaborative project organized by Andrew Wade and Andrew Nelson, the founders of the IMPACT Radiological Mummy Database[8]. The scans (converted from DICOM medical files to stereolithography files) were printed at John Abbott College to produce three rapid prototype models of the skulls found deep within the wrappings of the mummies for the purpose of facial reconstruction, which was undertaken by the Canadian forensic artist Victoria Lywood. The physical appearances of the deceased were reconstructed by arranging the hair in hairstyles that could be derived from the CT scans, inserting artificial eyes, or applying subcutaneous packing material [26].

Another project centered on the printing of a human skull was undertaken by the Richard III Society. The bones of the famous king where recently found in a car park [27], and were used to make a digital reconstruction of the king's head, using contemporary paintings and documents. This reconstruction was then 3D printed as a physical model, and has been exhibited in several venues throughout England [28].

Naturally, these printed models can only be as good as the reconstruction on the computer, but it is their physical presence, which makes them more 'real', and, in the opinion of some, more uncanny. Indeed, this technique is very similar to the famous wax cabinets, which have been used to preserve and illustrate the features of illustrious personalities for centuries.

Our own research on what we call Tactile Photography shall be mentioned in this context, too. The concept has been recently introduced in publications and at conferences, e.g. [29] and could become a new cross-over medium, for artistic creation as well as for accessible documentation in the field of cultural heritage.

Enhancing photography with the illusion of depth and physical space has been a long-lasting interest, embodied in techniques such as Multi-Photography [30], Peripheral Photography, Photostereo Synthesis and Photo Sculpture [31, 32]. The latter technique, originally invented in 1859 by the French sculptor and photographer François Willème, is the adaption of photographic portraits to the construction of three-dimensional portrait-sculptures. It is currently experiencing a renaissance via photogrammetry, triggered by Autodesk's 123D Catch Application[9] (formerly Project Photofly), which allows users to create 3D models from digital photographs, on their computer and even directly on smartphones.

---

[8] Website http://www.impactdb.uwo.ca
[9] Website http://www.123dapp.com

Fig. 4. Tactile Photography prototype. Source: [29]

Tactile Photography, however, is based on digital Stereoscopy, a technique that has recently entered the consumer market, in the form of digital "3D cameras" for photography, such as Fuji's FinePix REAL 3D model or similar 3D capturing techniques. What distinguishes Stereoscopy is its ability to capture not only color but to also encode the depth at every point, i.e., the plasticity, and the surface. This surface is recovered using photogrammetry and 3D printed in colored relief form. For certain kinds of documentation in cultural heritage, e.g. moving objects, which cannot be easily captured by multi-view photogrammetry, or simply because of its "point and shoot" character, Tactile Photography might be more suitable than freestanding 3D objects. Furthermore, it should be conceived as an easy-to-use and affordable technique, which could record additional information (e.g., sound) together with the digital photographs.

3.4   Public Outreach Activities

Public outreach seems to be even greater when 3D printing is involved as a *process*, not only as a *result* of the work of specialists in the field of cultural heritage. Educational activities, especially with young adults, such as the *Power of Making Workshops* in the Victoria & Albert Museum are excellent examples for a successful implementation of the Do-It-Yourself approach in the cultural field. The same is true for the *Makerspaces* at the Newark Museum, and the Art Institute of Chicago, to name just a few [33].

In 2012, the Metropolitan Museum of Art in New York organized its first 3D scanning and printing *Hackathon* [33, 34]. The invited guests spent several days photographing museum objects and converting the images into 3D models. The artworks are digitized by utilizing the free software called 123D Catch, which even runs on smartphones and tablets, already mentioned in the previous subsection.

Fig. 5. Conversion scheme of the sculpture "Leda and the Swan" into a 3D model (Source: [34]) and the 3D model on the Thingiverse Website[10]

The results were uploaded to Thingiverse.com, a collection of virtual models, for anyone to print them at home with a 3D printer. According to one of the participating digital artists, "the project effectively established a prototype for a new way of experiencing and sharing museum collections and artwork" [34].

Our own implementation for the MUSA Museum in Vienna in 2009 was a somewhat similar experiment: Our aim was to re-translate a photographic work by Lotte Hendrich-Hassmann back into the 3rd dimension. The original photograph stems from the documentation of the performance "Bilderschatten – Schattenbilder", staged by Rita Furrer, in the framework of a performance festival, which took place in Krems, Austria, in 1983 [35]. The setting of the performance was the secularized Dominican church, where Furrer installed six plaster castings of herself, which were covered with cloth, and then moved around them, in rhythmical movements. The photograph by her artist-colleague Hendrich-Hassmann shows one of the plaster sculptures, standing near to a massive column in the church. Once we decided to make the photograph accessible for tactile exploration, the options were a raised line diagram, a relief or – more daringly – a full 3D representation.

The creation of full 3D models from lower-dimensional input is technically and (conceptually) challenging, as backsides and hidden parts are not present in the input date and have to be completed or hallucinated [36, p. 500]. Only when additional knowledge or multiple views are available, the conversion is easier. We tackled the problem by restaging the scene with a human model in the same pose as the plaster cast on the photograph and created a 1:5 scale model of the human figure by means of

3D scanning and rapid prototyping technologies, undertaken at the Vienna University of Technology. The model was then covered with cloth and received a metal piece joining the arms, just as the original full-scale plaster model. The outcome was exhibited on a pedestal, next to the photograph, in the gallery space of the Museum auf Abruf (MUSA), with a wall label that indicated to the visitors that this object could be touched (cf. Fig. 3).

Another important project in this field is *Smart Replicas*, in which the Dutch design researcher Maaike Roozenburg is using 3D printing to create replicas of rare pieces of ceramics, and using an augmented reality application for smartphones to overlay animations and text, and even play music pieces that present the viewer with the object's historical context [37].

4   Guidelines, Standards and Evaluation Techniques in 3D Printing for Cultural Heritage

Despite of the new interest in multisensory experiences in the arts and the constantly growing number of possibilities in the field of additive manufacturing, there are still no common standards for tactile model making[11]. Also, few tools for 3D scanning, photogrammetry and modeling take the necessities of both the field of cultural heritage and accessibility matters into account. And as no specialized education exists, the interpretation artists[12] tend to bring their own individual intuition and experiences from other fields into the process, which leads to a myriad of highly creative and interesting approaches, but no common standards can be developed.

Another important issue is the storage of such 3D models in digital libraries, especially the questions where and how to archive them, in which file format and under which license. The results of the above mentioned Hackathon at the Metropolitan Museum were uploaded to Thingiverse.com in the STL file format and "licensed under the Creative Commons - Attribution - Share Alike license" [34].

Challenges also emerge from the need to create tools, standards and a basic curriculum for those artists engaged in the use of 3D Printing in cultural heritage, taking multi-sensory interpretation and accessibility matters into account. Furthermore, extensive testing and evaluation of the different approaches and production techniques for 3D printed models will be necessary.

---

[11] However, there are some specific guidelines for the production of diagrams on paper for the visually impaired, such as *Tactile Diagrams* [13] created by the Art Beyond Sight Foundation, Yvonne Eriksson's *How to make tactile pictures understandable to the blind reader* [38], and the *Guidelines and Standards for Tactile Graphics* [39]. While these are all purpose-built for visually impaired users, they could serve well as examples, if taken to a more general level and combined with the Design For All philosophy.

[12] These artists, who normally have undergone an education in sculpture, design or crafts, are also sometimes referred to as conversion artists. Some of them also create building models, and vice versa, even if these model makers generally have an education in architecture or design.

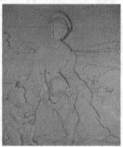

Fig. 6. Evaluation Process of *Tactile Paintings* (Source: [36])

This evaluation should include testing against traditional model making in clay and with computer-aided machining approaches, and should allow refining the list of restrictions, tools and possibilities for 3D Printing in the cultural heritage domain.

In test settings, blind and visually impaired test persons often point out that verbal description is still most important in order to get the context, background information and guidance while touching [36, p. 503]. The chosen materials for 3D Printing have to be pleasant to the touch but easy to clean and robust. Using different materials as for the original objects is often unavoidable. The original material should at least be easy to imagine from verbal description or material samples. Yet, it is often beneficial to have replicas in a similar texture, weight and materiality. Having a wider range of materials for additive manufacturing, as well as machines that can print colored surfaces on these materials would be a great improvement in this context. Of course, these properties should be reflected as metadata, especially the choice of material of the tactile model. One could even think of a classification of these materials in the form of a thesaurus or code, in the style of the Pantone code for colors.

An even broader range of possibilities is to be expected in the field of interactive multi-sensorial exploration. 3D objects could be enriched by auditory or other sensory information, triggered by touch, voice or other gestures, much like 2D information kiosks nowadays, but directly on the 3D objects. Research questions arise concerning output possibilities, content generation, authoring and gesture detection.

Finger-tracking and gesture-recognition techniques [40] are readily available in 2D media and graphics tablets, and tactile 2D graphic displays such as the HyperBraille tablet [41] have integrated touch sensors over their whole surface. For 3D objects, one possibility is to apply conductive paint on important parts that register touch events [42]. An interesting development would be 3D printing techniques that could directly embed conductive parts. However, this technique is limited to recognize touch on only a few areas (hotspots). A more versatile and fine-grained approach is 3D finger tracking, but this has not yet been applied to object touch recognition, apart from a small study [43]. Recent sensor developments, like Microsoft's Kinect sensor [44], could make the task of finger tracking much easier. These sensors have been specifically developed for body tracking, by sensing a depth video image in addition to a color video. The sensor is comparatively inexpensive, and its finger-tracking capabilities have already been demonstrated [45]. Future work in this field should extend these finger-tracking capabilities with object tracking in order to locate the finger relative to the object to be touched, resulting in a high-resolution tracking device, which works on the surfaces of 3D printed objects, and will be a flexible tool for position-specific information retrieval.

5   Conclusion

Available scanning, Rapid Prototyping, and especially 3D Printing technologies offer great opportunities to bring back multi-sensory and especially haptic experiences into our cultural heritage, without compromising conservational concerns. Objects can be reconstructed from pieces, mummies hidden in their enclosures can be made visible and tangible without destruction, and exhibits can be placed into their appropriate context. Through institutional effort but also through crowd-sourcing activities, large collections can be made available to everyone with access to internet and 3D printing facilities.

The ability to bring objects into an appropriate scale, to enhance tactile features and to translate non-tactile features for easier perception may even enrich experiences beyond the original objects. In the context of the Design for All philosophy, all people benefit from these enhancements, especially people that could not fully appreciate the original objects, like blind or visually impaired visitors, people with learning disabilities, children, or elderly people.

However, no standards for the translation into multi-sensory 3D objects yet exist which guarantee an optimal information transfer. Possibilities need to be researched, tested and codified, and finally conversion artists trained. In terms of technology, affordable and easy-to-use scanning and reproduction methods will be further developed, and a wider range of durable and optimally full-color materials for 3D Printing will hopefully be found, making this field, and its applications for cultural heritage, even more exciting as it is today.

References

1. The Economist, Print me a Stradivarius. How a new manufacturing technology will change the world, pp. 12–18 (February 2011)
2. Bickel, B., Bächer, M., Otaduy, M., Lee, H.R., Pfister, H., Gross, M., Matusik, W.: Design and Fabrication of Materials with Desired Deformation Behavior. In: Proceedings of ACM SIGGRAPH, Los Angeles, USA, July 25-29 (2010), ACM Transactions on Graphics 29(3), 63:1–63:10 (2010)
3. Elkins, J.: On Some Limits of Materiality. ArtHistory, Das Magazin des Instituts für Theorie (Special issue on 'Taktilität: Sinneserfahrung als Grenzerfahrung') 31, 25–30 (2008)

4. Hospers, J.: The Philosophy of Art. In: Encyclopedia Britannica, http://global.britannica.com/EBchecked/topic/36433/art-philosophy-of
5. Greenberg, C.: Towards a Newer Laocoon. Partisan Review VII(4), 296–310 (1940)
6. Classen, C., Howes, D.: The Museum as Sensescape: Western Sensibilities and Indigenous Artifacts. In: Engaging All the Senses: Colonialism, Processes of Perception and the Status of Artifacts, Wenner-Gren Foundation for Anthropological Research, Sintra, September 26 - October 2 (2003)
7. Paul, C.: Digital Art. Thames & Hudson, London (2003)
8. Krauss, R.: A Voyage in the North Sea. Art in the Age of the Post-Medium Condition. Thames & Hudson, London (1999)
9. Manovich, L.: Post-Media Aesthetics (originally 2001, yet the text is being adapted over the years and is online in its latest version), http://manovich.net/content/04-projects/029-post-media-aesthetics/29_article_2001.pdf
10. Grau, O. (ed.): Media Art Histories. MIT-Press, Cambridge (2007)
11. Rath, M., Trempler, J., Wenderholm, I. (eds.): Das haptische Bild, Körperhafte Bilderfahrung in der Neuzeit. Akademieverlag, Berlin (forthcoming)
12. O'Neill, P., Wilson, M. (eds.): Curating and the Educational Turn. Open Editions: Occasional Table Critical Series. De Appel, Amsterdam (2010)
13. Axel, E., Levent, N. (eds.): Art Beyond Sight: A Resource Guide to Art, Creativity and Visual Impairment. AFB Press, New York (2002)
14. Ioannides, M., Arnold, D.B., Niccolucci, F., Mania, F. (eds.): Proceedings of VAST 2006: The 7th International Symposium on Virtual Reality, Archaeology and Intelligent Cultural Heritage, Nicosia, Cyprus. Eurographics Association (2006)
15. Knapp, M., Wolff, R., Lipson, H. : Developing printable content: A repository for printable teaching models. In: Proceedings of the 19th Annual Solid Freeform Fabrication Symposium, Austin TX, USA (2008), http://creativemachines.cornell.edu/papers/SFF08_Knapp.pdf
16. Kuchenbecker, K.J., Romano, J., McMahan, W.: Haptography: Capturing and recreating the rich feel of real surfaces. In: Pradalier, C., Siegwart, R., Hirzinger, G. (eds.) Invited paper at the International Symposium on Robotics Research, Berlin and Heidelberg, August 2009. Springer Tracts in Advanced Robotics, vol. 70 (2011)
17. Design For All Foundation Website, Section: What is Design For All?, http://www.designforall.org/en/dfa/dfa.php
18. Acuity Design Blog, http://acuitydesign.blogspot.co.uk/2013/03/photocopying-past.html
19. Learning Site web page, http://www.learningsites.com/Nuzi/Nuzi_images/LSInc_NuziLion_02.pdf, http://www.learningsites.com/Frame_layout01.htm
20. Fujiwara, D.: 3D Printing Pivotal to Forbidden City Extreme Makeover (April 14, 2012), http://3dprinterhub.com/3d-printer-news/3d-printing-pivotal-to-forbidden-city-extreme-makeover/169/
21. Gangjee, N., Lipson, H., Owen, D.I.: 3D Printing of Cuneiform Tablets. Cornell Creative Machines Lab, http://creativemachines.cornell.edu/cuneiform
22. Reichinger, A., Maierhofer, S., Purgathofer, W.: High-Quality Tactile Paintings. Journal on Computing and Cultural Heritage 4(2), 5:1–5:13 (2011)
23. Shift in Perspectives. Arts and Disability Ireland, Dublin (2010)

24. Terdiman, D.: Smithsonian turns to 3D to bring collection to the world. CNET (February 24, 2012), http://news.cnet.com/8301-13772_3-57384166-52/smithsonian-turns-to-3d-to-bring-collection-to-the-world/
25. Video posted on May 13, 2013, by YouTube user SmithsonianVideos, http://www.youtube.com/watch?v=AWoqTGEw7WA
26. Lywood, V.: The Mummies at Redpath Museum, http://www.victorialywood.com/The_Mummies.html
27. Buckley, R., Morris, M., Appleby, J., King, T., O'Sullivan, D., Foxhall, L.: The king in the car park: new light on the death and burial of Richard III in the Grey Friars church, Leicester, in 1485. Antiquity 87(336), 519–538 (2013)
28. Garber, M.: The Uncanny Face Model They Made With Richard III's Skull... And it was made by, yep, a 3D printer. In The Atlantic (May 17, 2013), http://www.theatlantic.com/technology/archive/2013/05/the-uncanny-face-model-they-made-with-richard-iiis-skull/275965/
29. Neumüller, M., Reichinger, A.: From Stereoscopy to Tactile Photography. In: PhotoResearcher No 19, Vienna, pp. 59-63 (April 2013)
30. Blunck, L.: Chimären im Spiegel. Anmerkungen zur sogenannten Multifotografie, Fotogeschichte 94, 3–14 (2004)
31. Schmidt, G.: Die Simultaneität der Blicke. Über ein medientechnisches Dispositiv. In: Visualisierungen des Ereignisses. Kultur- und Medientheorie, Berlin (2009)
32. Beckmann, A.: Fotoskulptur. Überlegungen zu einem Bildmedium des 19. Jahrhunderts. Fotogeschichte 39, 3–16 (1991)
33. Neely, L., Langer, M.: Please Feel the Museum: The Emergence of 3D Printing and Scanning. Museums and the Web 2013, Conference, Portland, OR, USA, April 17-20 (2013), http://mw2013.museumsandtheweb.com/paper/please-feel-the-museum-the-emergence-of-3d-printing-and-scanning/
34. Monaghan, J.: Metropolitan Museum 3D Hackathon (June 2012), http://jonmonaghan.com/research/metropolitan-museum-3d-hackathon/
35. Aigner, S., Karel, J. (eds.): Raum Körpereinsatz, Positionen der Skulptur. Verlag Moderne Kunst, Nürnberg (2010)
36. Reichinger, A., Neumüller, M., Rist, F., Maierhofer, S., Purgathofer, W.: Computer-Aided Design of Tactile Models. In: Miesenberger, K., Karshmer, A., Penaz, P., Zagler, W. (eds.) ICCHP 2012, Part II. LNCS, vol. 7383, pp. 497–504. Springer, Heidelberg (2012)
37. Roozenburg, M.: Smart Replicas: bringing heritage back to life. Presentation at Smart Replicas at MuseumNext Conference Fringe Symposium (May 13, 2013), http://smartreplicas.blogspot.com.es/2013/05/smart-replicas-at-museumnext-fringe.html
38. Eriksson, Y.: How to make tactile pictures understandable to the blind reader. IFLA/SLB Pre-conference Seminar in Penang (1999), http://archive.ifla.org/IV/ifla65/65ye-e.htm
39. Braille Authority of North America and Canadian Braille Authority:Guidelines and Standards for Tactile Graphics (2010). Web Version February 2012, http://www.brailleauthority.org/tg/web-manual/index.html
40. Vlaming, L.: Human Interfaces – Finger Tracking Applications. Department of Computer Science, University of Groningen (2008)
41. Hyperbraille Project, http://www.hyperbraille.de/

42. Touch Graphic's Touch Sensor, http://touchgraphics.com/OnlineStore/index.php/tactile-materials/touchsensor.html

43. Seisenbacher, G., Mayer, P., Panek, P., Zagler, W.L.: 3D-Finger - System for Auditory Support of Haptic Exploration in the Education of Blind and Visually Impaired Students - Idea and Feasibility Study. In: Assistive Technology from Virtuality to Reality. IOS Press, Amsterdam (2005)

44. Giles, J.: Inside the Race to Hack the Kinect. The New Scientist, 208(2789) (2010), http://www.newscientist.com/article/dn19762-inside-the-race-to-hack-the-kinect.html

45. Kinecthacks   Demonstration,   http://www.kinecthacks.com/image-manipulation-with-kinect-finger-tracking

3D Reconstruction from 3D Cultural Heritage Models

Patrick Callet

Ecole Centrale Paris, Applied Maths and Systems, grande voie des vignes,
92290 Châtenay-Malabry, France
Mines Paris-Tech, Centre de Robotique, 60 bd. Saint Michel,
75006 Paris, France
vice-président du Centre Français de la Couleur
patrick.callet@ecp.fr

Abstract. 3D data acquisition and 3D virtual and physical reproductions are shortly described within the framework of our experiments with museum artefacts. Our experience in the cultural heritage field illustrates a lot of problems encountered and the solutions we brought. From this short analysis, a perspective for the next 10 or 20 years is sketched. There are many difficulties, either scientific or technological. We point out some of them that seem to be very important in the to domains of science and technology. Thus we describe emerging activities in the scientific domain where Spectroscopic Ellipsometry is now starting for the spectral acquisition of very accurate optical data on materials, i.e. complex indices of refraction. Surprisingly inverse methods should also appear with the difficulty to 3D capture a material shape very glossy, transparent or translucent. The text provides many examples and, among them, the rendering and making of the famous tablet of Idalion.

Keywords: Spectrophotometry, goniospectrophotometry, spectroscopic ellispsometry, spectral rendering, virtual metallurgy, stained-glass window, natural lighting.

1   Introduction

Related to the work flow from 3D data acquisition to the 3D virtual and physical reproduction we present some aspects of an historical and recent scientific activity. Our experience in the cultural heritage field illustrates a lot of problems encountered and the solutions we brought. This short analysis providing a perspective for the next 10 or 20 years is sketched. There are many difficulties, either scientific or technological. We point out some of them that seem to be very important in the domains of science and technology. Thus we describe emerging activities in the scientific domain where Spectroscopic Ellipsometry is now starting for the spectral acquisition of very accurate optical data on materials, i.e. complex indices of refraction. Surprisingly inverse methods should also appear with the difficulty to 3D capture a material shape very glossy, transparent or translucent. All these methods must be applied without any contact with the original artifact. Thus we can imagine the simultaneous development of scientific approaches useful for spectral rendering

M. Ioannides and E. Quak (Eds.): 3D Research Challenges, LNCS 8355, pp. 135–142, 2014.

and applied methods for 3D shape acquisition. The text is illustrated with many examples and, among them, the rendering and making of the famous tablet of Idalion.

2   Scanning and Measurement Tools

There is not enough space here to describe each technical processes used in 3D shape acquisition. We only describe one of the most "promising" developments for the next years. The common fundamental tool used for 3D scanning and measurement is light itself. Obviously, the main advantage is in case of archaeological objects, any direct physical contact is forbidden. However, if such a use becomes more and more frequent, possible induced damages when using light sources (laser and others) is still not studied enough. For painted works, this may have in some circumstances, even at very low intensity and short time exposures, a significant effect on chromatic properties (pigments modification and chemical induced reactions, etc.).

Fig. 1. Left: One of the first 3D scanning devices in the world created in 1988 by Francis Schmitt at ENST in Paris. The trace of the illumination plane produced by a He-Ne laser source is viewed and recorded by a monochrome camera. Right: Brass statuette of the "Dieu guerrier gaulois de Saint-Maur en chaussée" and the scanning setup.

2.1   Shape Acquisition

In shape measurements, the main commonly used tools are laser scanners, structured light devices, photogrammetry, photomodeling, etc. These tools are able to provide very large data sets, clouds of points, images, etc. possibly organized or not. An historical example of a scanning device is given in Fig. 1.

The impact on the computing resources and necessary storage availabilities is then more and more important. Computer scientists are working along with art historians, archaeologists, chemists, physicists, engineers, etc. as interdisciplinarity is now indispensable. The inherent limitation in shape acquisition depends on the accuracy of object surface definition. Many objects are corroded or oxidized, hence it is difficult to delimit where the "good shape", the meaningful one, is. In practice, the surface is scaled to the optical appearance of the shape as recorded by the optical device. The surface definition, even with spatial sampling and accuracy problems, depends on the wavelength used and the state of the surface, itself depending on the materials nearest to the surface. At this scale of measurements, the recorded, approximated surface, describes "waviness" and "roughness". Waviness, e.g. brush prints on a painting, may be confused with the digital noise inherent to the acquisition process, while roughness depends on the wavelength. To avoid confusion between the two kinds of effects a special signal treatment has to be carried out on the whole data set. The roughness estimation is generally obtained on a characteristic part of the object and measured by laser profilometry (often using a unique wavelength).

2.2   Optical Properties Acquisition

Transparency, high reflectivity, opalescence, glazes, varnishes, enamels, are few examples of the difficulties encountered with light and materials to be 3D digitized:. As the interaction of light with materials is influenced by the shape and optical appearance properties all the modes of the interaction must be considered. This is necessary, not only for the reproduction of the appearance of today but essential to retrieve previous aspects corresponding to a period when the object or monument was in use. Non-invasive techniques are used to characterize the materials contributing to the optical appearance. Spectrophotometric measurements, giving diffuse reflection or transmission spectra are commonly used. Thus accurate measurements are useful but generally cannot be performed on a large part of the object. Some techniques, based on high definition images, need 10 to 20 spectral images to identify the surface materials responsible for color appearance. The glossy and colored materials require the identification of the complex index of refraction of the object's surface most external layer. When some special physical measurements that provide the composition of the surface material are available, a reconstruction of the optical properties limited to a part of the object, is possible. A full spectral scanning of an artefact is no longer an inaccessible dream. Physics and more computing will lead to new hypotheses about the original appearance of a monument or an object. It is not often possible to get the required information about the materials without taking directly some takings of the original object. Today, many scientific instruments are more and more portable and can reach the museums or archaeological sites without the problem of artwork transportation, protection and conservation. For underwater acquisition, the only system used today is photogrammetry. In aerial sites many different devices are used today, depending on the size of the object to be digitized.

3   Replication Tools

3D digitization inherently produces some special noises due to systematic and repetitive scanning process. For instance, in 2003 we worked on a buddha head from Afghanistan displayed at the National Museum of Asian Art-Guimet, in Paris. It was necessary to physically replicate the statue for a humanitarian action within the framework of a scholarship project in Kabul. The result from 3D scanning was visualized throught , our free spectral simulation software Virtuelium (Fig. 2).

Fig. 2. The 3D reconstruction of the buddha head obtained by a Breuckmann structured light device. Spectral simulation with our free software "Virtuelium" (see www.virtuelium.free.fr).

The digital replica was acceptable with the prints of the scanning process but these technological traces had to be removed for the physical replicas. From the 3D cloud of points a first physical prototype was made in stereophotolithography resin polymerized by a UV laser. We then obtained a very beautiful object while the stratified structure appeared excessively. From this positive shape we made a silicone mould (Fig. 3) useful for a unique plaster replica. At this step, a sculptor had to remove our technological and very regular prints on the statue's surface without removing the alteration prints of the original. This differentiation was made using photographs of the original, taken at the museum. In the last step we made a new mould by physical contact with the artist's "corrected plaster". This last mould is used to produce a lot of patinated plaster replicas soldfor the benefice of the French humanitarian association "Afghanistan Demain". The above technique of replication is one of the two general methods of sculpture: material deposition or material removal. The acquired 3D data may be used for driving a digital robot (milling machine). It is clear that these data with appropriate devices may be employed for scaling the replicated object for various purposes. The beautiful exhibition in Rome (2003-2005) "I colori del bianco" displayed some polychrome replicas of antique sculptures in marble. Original sculptures with only tiny polychromy remains were compared to their replicas at the size and material (white marble). Replicas were colored with the identified pigments analyzed on the basis of the original remains. A second example, this time with no color, can be given. Rapid prototyping by milling is employed for the restoration of the Parthenon in Athens. The direct digitization on site of the damaged parts (digital stamping analogous in principle to the use of clay and plaster) is immediately used for the replication in marble at the same scale. Thus an excellent and morphological joint is obtained and the whole building retrieves its original shape, rendered with good material and an excellent mechanical behavior.

It is generally admitted that a replica cannot be produced in the same material as the original. This is only attempted by falsifiers. In spite of this deontological aspect we decided together with our colleagues in France and Cyprus to replicate the so important piece of the cypriot history in the same material and at the same scale:

the tablet of Idalion. This replica of the antique bronze, accurately modelled at 40 μm in spatial resolution, was offered to Cyprus during the EuroMed conference in 2010 in Limassol. We then decided two important issues to notify that this accurate replica differs from the original piece in Paris (National Library of France). The first decision was to leave the technological prints due to the rapid prototyping involving the modern wax prepared for bronze casting. The second was to engrave on an edge "Bibliothèque Nationale de France". In Fig. 4 the spectrally computed image of the Idalion tablet according to its bronze composition is presented.

Fig. 3. The first mould in silicone (2003) produced for the plaster replication of the buddha head from Afghanistan (III-IVth c. AC). The concave shape of the mould is lighted from,the back so that it appears orange-golden. The lighter parts are due to the smallest thickness of the silicone. Observed by reflection, the material appears milky, depending on the local thickness. The technological prints are quite visible on the whole face ; they have to be removed before making the final mould for casting the plaster replicas.

One of the advantages of making an accurate replica (in shape and material) lies in the ability to have the original optical aspect while the original artefact is only viewed with the patination historically developed until today (Fig. 5). The ageing of materials is also concerned here when comparing originals and replicas. The computational tools will have to account for these difficulties.

We also previously worked [1] on the concept of Virtual Metallurgy in 2002-2005 and studied a first category of alloys that were made in Mesopotamy. Silver-Lead alloys appeared as very original materials with optical properties that were unimaginable without physics and spectral computing techniques. The most original contribution and scientific way to solve similar problems was to find the optical constants of all the compounds. These so-called "constants" are in reality wavelength dependent. They are measured by spectroscopic ellipsometry (SE) [2]. As this method is very fruitful we always use SE for bronze or in a general setting, not only for binary alloys. We then possess a collection of complex indices of refraction very characteristic of the material to render in spectral simulation. For example a virtual shader is presented in Fig. 6 and represent the optical properties of various bronzes according to their composition.

Fig. 4. Spectral simulation of the tablet of Idalion computed with Virtuelium obtained in normalized conditions (CIE D65 illuminant, CIE 1964 10° observer)

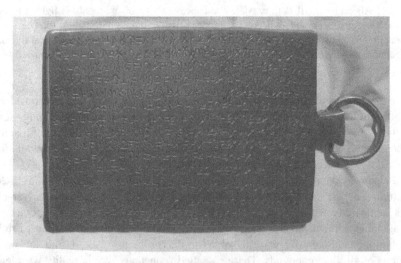

Fig. 5. The physical replica of the tablet of Idalion (Cyprus) in bronze obtained by casting

Fig. 6. The virtual shader of bronze computed with the complex indices of refraction acquired by spectroscopic ellipsometry and according to the real composition of tin (Sn) and copper Cu)

4   New Problems and Future Research

The above description of the pertinent data useful for spectral imaging and retrieving the lost aspects of artefacts or monuments will progress in the direction of acquisition of more and more accurate 3D shapes and optical data which, for several reasons, will involve Spectroscopic Ellipsometry. First, for representing today's state of the scanned objects but also for obtaining a vision of their use in natural or anthropogenic lighting conditions. This is the way to include optical anisotropy of materials at a very "intimate" scale in the meaning of WYSIWYG (What You See Is What You Get). The technological developments will also reach more spectral display systems so that the accurate optical data will lead to very new visions of the past. Rapid prototyping tools use more and more color capabilities to render what was measured or computed from chemical or optical analysis. Some inherent difficulties appear to be linked to the metamerism problem lying in the pigment manufacturing technology (too many "constant-in-mean" diameters) so that the shades are too pale regarding to those obtained by the handcrafted grinding of natural pigments. Frescoes and gilts, silver-gold plating, gems, etc. are also of interest in this framework.

This scientific field concerns lighting and the systematic study of local environment when possible. To retrieve lighting conditions from the ancient time we have to consider the precession of the equinoxes and the water levels of rivers, lakes or seas. For instance, the indirect lighting condition due to theses situations is important for caves lighting that depends on solar orientation and reflection of the environment.

5   Conclusion

Using some examples stemming from previous works, we described how optical appearance rendering or retrieval of a 3D shape mainly depends on the performance of technologies used in data acquisition. It generally focuses on 3D digitization for the virtual and trichromatic restitution of existing objects in their nowadays state. This approach is very limited when we are concerned with previous state of objects; this is another way to understand the past and the use, symbolic or not, of objects in different periods and locations. The future will have to solve complex optical problems both in digitization and rendering. In fact the two necessary ways to follow are closely linked.

The use of light polarization in the rendering process of transparent or translucent materials would be very useful to the design of scanning devices for the same materials that are today excluded [3]. Transparency, translucence, shininess, glossiness, etc. are complicated scientific fields and will lead to great challenges in the coming years.

References

1. Callet, P., Zymla, A.: Rendering of binary alloys – Example and validation with bronze. In: Proc. 2nd Int. Conf. Comp. Vision Graphics, ICCVG 2004. Springer, Warsaw (2005)
2. Callet, P., de Contencin, F.-X., Zymla, A., Denizet, P., Hilpert, T., Miyazawa, K., Robin, B.: An emblematic bronze from Cyprus the Idalion project. In: Ioannides, M., Fellner, D., Georgopoulos, A., Hadjimitsis, D.G. (eds.) EuroMed 2010. LNCS, vol. 6436, pp. 206–224. Springer, Heidelberg (2010)
3. Callet, P.: From fundamental optical properties of materials to visual appearance: metals, alloys, gilts, glasses, paints, photonics and biophotonics. In: VIIIth Color Conference, Alma Mater Studorium, Università di Bologna, Italy (2012)

Author Index

Callet, Patrick   135
Callieri, Marco   18
Cignoni, Paolo   18

Dellepiane, Matteo   18
De Luca, Livio   36
Di Benedetto, Marco   18
Dodgson, Neil A.   93

Fellner, Dieter   1, 64

Garcia, Ander   104

Havemann, Sven   64

Juaristi, Miriam   104

Kern, Christian   119

Linaza, Maria Teresa   104
Lo Buglio, David   36

Maïm, Barbara   78
Maïm, Jonathan   78
Malomo, Luigi   18

Neumüller, Moritz   119

Pena Serna, Sebastian   1
Ponchio, Federico   18

Reichinger, Andreas   119
Rist, Florian   119

Santos, Pedro   1
Scopigno, Roberto   18
Stork, André   1

Tal, Ayellet   50
Thalmann, Daniel   78

Wagener, Olaf   64

Printed in the United States
By Bookmasters